THE PICK OF THE SEASON

A Comedy in Three Acts

By JEAN McCONNELL

Cressrelles Publishing Co Ltd

10 Station Road Industrial Estate, Colwall,
Herefordshire WR14 6RN *Telephone:* 01684 540154

ACTING FEES FOR PERFORMANCES OVERSEAS

Apply to : **South Africa**: Mello House, PO Box 236, Sea Point 8060, Capetown. **Kenya**: National Theatre, PO Box 452, Nairobi. **Southern Rhodesia**: Association of Rhodesian Theatrical Soc., PO Box 2701, Salisbury. **Australia**: Will Andrade, 275c Pitt Street, Sydney, NSW, Australia 2000. **New Zealand**: Play Bureau, Box 3611, Wellington. **Canada & U.S.A.**: Walter H. Baker Co., Boston. **Holland**: International Bureau, Vondelstraat 102, Amsterdam.

The action of the play takes place in the large kitchen of a farmhouse in Kent

CHARACTERS

SUNNY FINCHER

FRED FINCHER, his son

ROSE FINCHER, Fred's wife

MARY FINCHER, their daughter

NORMAN BATES

MRS. CARRAWAY

DOLLY FAGG, her daughter

A FARMHAND

THE PICK OF THE SEASON

A Comedy in Three Acts

By JEAN McCONNELL

ACT I.

The scene is the large kitchen of a farmhouse in Kent. There is a door D.R. *to the dining room, another* U.R. *to the scullery, and a staircase* U.L. *An old-fashioned range stands* L. *with a chair downstage and a desk and chair upstage of it. There is a dresser* R. *and pot with hydrangea below it. At back there is a window and an open door through which can be seen* SUNNY FINCHER, *sitting outside in the garden. He is in his seventies and is chatting to his bulbs as he plants them in pots. There is another chair near the centre of the room by a table at which stands* ROSE FINCHER, *who is in her forties, plump and good-natured. She is making bread rolls, but her thoughts are far away and somewhat troubled.*

It is an early evening in late August.

After a moment MARY FINCHER *is seen coming through the garden. She is a spirited, attractive girl. As she reaches* SUNNY *she pauses.*

SUNNY. 'Allo, Mary, back already! (*To bulb*). That's right, my pretty, tuck up snug with your brothers.

MARY. Hullo Grandad!

SUNNY. You come and see what I'm doin'. (*To bulb*). Naow don't pretend I'm 'urtin' you 'cause I wouldn't do a thing like that.

MARY. Tulip bulbs?

SUNNY. That's right. 'Ave some Christmas maybe. (*To bulb*). What about it, eh? (*To Mary*). Isn't 'e a beauty?

MARY. Yes. Is that bit sticking up the *top* end?

SUNNY. That's right, my dear. Make a gardener of you yet, we will.

MARY. Well in that case, you've got all the others in upside down!

SUNNY. Eh? 'Ere, where are my glasses?

MARY. (*Putting them on his nose*). Here.

SUNNY. Mm. You're right.

MARY. You shouldn't work without them.

SUNNY. Mm. (*Picking up an object*). One of them ain't even a tulip—'tis a doorknob! (*He tosses it away*).

(MARY *passes into the kitchen*).

ROSE. Oh, there you are, Mary. Er—Mary, are you doin' anythin' for a minute?

MARY. No Mum, but I'm going out soon.

ROSE. Well, I want to talk to you. I've—I've had a letter.

MARY. A letter?

ROSE. From old Mrs. Carraway. (MARY *looks surprised*). Well, from Mrs. Fagg her daughter really—but about Mrs. Carraway. I don't know how I'm going to tell your father.

MARY. Tell him what?

ROSE. Shut the door a minute, dear. Grandad's sure to go blurtin' it out if he hears and I want to tell Fred in my own time.

MARY. (*Closing garden door*). What's the mystery?

ROSE. Oh, it's nothing much really. It's just that—well I suppose I should have told everyone before.

MARY. What have you been up to, Mum?

ROSE. Don't put it like that, Mary. It was just a simple letter—very badly spelled too. Your father saw it, as a matter of fact.

MARY. Well, if he saw it—

ROSE. Oh, but not inside it, he didn't. He thought it was just asking us to reserve them a bin for the hop pickin', same as usual. He just took a glance at the envelope and threw it aside, saying, 'those damned Carraways!'

MARY. I don't know why he lets them come every year when he hates them so much.

ROSE. He really couldn't do anythin' else, Mary. There've been Carraways coming down hoppin' for so long. There were Carraways pickin' at this farm long before our time.

MARY. That sort of thing doesn't usually bother Dad.

ROSE. Now you mustn't say that, Mary. Your father has as fine feeling as anyone else. He's a kind and generous man deep down. And no-one can say Fred Fincher ever did anyone the least harm, except in fun. As a husband, deep down he's been a good-natured, loving—

MARY. What about the letter?

ROSE. (*Frowning*). Of course he has got a bit of a temper.

MARY. Not so deep down! What was in the letter anyway?

ROSE. The Carraways want to come and stay here.

MARY. (*Astounded*). To do what? In this house?

ROSE. Yes.

MARY. Why, Dad does nothing but have rows with them when they're miles away across the fields in a hut!

ROSE. I know. That's why I didn't show him the letter.

MARY. I should think not! Whatever made them suggest such an idea anyway?

ROSE. It's old Mrs. Carraway—she's not been at all well, it seems.

MARY. Golly! I can't imagine her ever having anything wrong with her.

ROSE. Well, she's gettin' on, you know.

MARY. She always looks so tough. I think it's the tattoo marks up her arms. When I was little I used to think she was a sort of lady pirate.

ROSE. Your dad doesn't think she's a lady anything! Anyway her daughter—

MARY. Mrs. Fagg?

ROSE. (*Nodding*). Doesn't think the old lady ought to sleep out in a hut this year. She says she's tried to stop her comin' but it just leads to scenes.

MARY. I'll bet!

ROSE. So she's managed to make her promise that if she comes down she'll stay in a proper house.

MARY. Maybe there'd be room for her in one of the cottages.

ROSE. No. She said she'd written round to some of the people here and no-one seemed able to take them.

MARY. I'm not really surprised.

ROSE. There's only the two of them comin' this year. Mrs. Fagg and the old woman.

MARY. And it doesn't look as if they're coming either. You didn't really mean to suggest it to Dad, did you?

ROSE. I—I don't know.

MARY. Oh ho! Let me be there!

ROSE. It was a very moving letter. All smudged.

MARY. She probably spilt her beer on it.

ROSE. No. She seemed very worried about old Mrs. Carraway. Said she was absolutely determined to come down. (*She produces a letter from her pocket and reads*). She finishes up: "Any sort of shake-down will do. The old girl's driving me crackers."

MARY. Well, it can't be helped. We can't do anything about it.

ROSE. We have got room.

MARY. We've got lots of room. We've also got Dad!

ROSE. He knows they're good pickers.

MARY. He wouldn't consider it.

ROSE. He needn't really see much of them—after all we'll be working all day.

MARY. He'll never agree.

ROSE. They could have their meals at different times.

MARY. It's no use, Mum. Dad wouldn't let them set foot in this house, you know he wouldn't. And you'll be asking for trouble to mention it.

ROSE. But they've always come!

MARY. And they've always had a row with dad!

ROSE. (*looking at the letter*). Then you definitely think I should say 'no.'

MARY. Definitely.

ROSE. Oh.

MARY. I'm going up to change, Mum. (*She moves to stairs*).

ROSE. Well, I've said 'yes.'

(*Mary stops dead*).

MARY. (*Returning*). You mean they're coming here?

ROSE. (*Producing another letter*). I had a letter from them yesterday.

MARY. (*Taking it and reading*). " Dear Mrs. Fincher, Very glad you can take us. We're coming down a week earlier like you said.

Reckon it will do ma good the few days rest though she is still on about sleeping in the hut but I'm being firm and the doctor says so too. Probably be down Tuesday all being well. Many thanks. Dolly Fagg." And you haven't even mentioned it to Dad?

ROSE. (*Shaking her head*). I've been tryin' to think of a way to break it.

MARY. Just tell him. He'll do the breaking!

ROSE. (*Agitated*). Maybe if they stayed in their room till he'd gone out in the morning and then at night I could put a light in the window when it was all clear to come in.

MARY. But what would they do? Wait about in the hedges until Dad went to bed? That'll do poor old Mrs. Carraway a lot of good.

ROSE. Yes. That won't do obviously. I've just got to tell Fred, that's all there is to it. After all we've had people stayin' before.

MARY. Not Carraways we haven't!

ROSE. And really we don't know them all that well. They're probably very nice.

MARY. Oh I expect they are—deep down! Don't worry, Mum, Dad won't eat you.

ROSE. I know that—but there's no tellin' what he'd do with a Carraway!

MARY. (*Moving to stairs*). Well, let me know when you tackle the the subject. No, don't bother—I'll know all right!

(*She ascends a few stairs, then returns*).

MARY. Wait a minute, when did they say they were coming?

ROSE. Tuesday. A week before the pickin' starts.

MARY. (*After a second's pause*). That was yesterday!

ROSE. Yes. I nearly died every time there was a knock. They'll probably come today.

MARY. Mum, you simply must tell Dad before they arrive!

ROSE. (*Worried*). I know. I'll tell him as soon as he comes in. I really will.

MARY. (*Ascending stairs*). You know your trouble is you're too easy-going. You're always afraid to speak up for yourself. Look how you get treated in the stool-ball team for instance.

ROSE. I play every week!

MARY. Well, I don't call it playing—when you never get the chance to bat. You know what's wrong with you? You let people walk all over you!

(*She disappears upstairs*).

ROSE. (*To herself*). Yes, I do! I ought to have more spirit! (*She squares her shoulders*). Now listen, Fred! (*She adopts an aggressive pose*). I don't care what you say, Fred! (*She goes on silently mouthing an argument—and getting the better of it.*).

MARY. (*Calling furiously over the bannisters*). Mum! You haven't washed my nylons!

ROSE. Well, I—.

MARY. You knew I wanted them! I've simply got to have some

decent ones. Look, if I bring them down would you do it now? There's just about time if we dry them over the stove and—

ROSE. (*Firmly*). Wear another pair!

MARY. What?

ROSE. (*With a little less conviction*). Wear another pair!

MARY. (*Meekly*), Oh. All right. (*She disappears*).

ROSE. (*Delighted*). Mm. It works! Wear another pair! Fred, I'm havin' my own way over this! Hm. (*She kneads her dough with abandon. Then taking up two stool-bats she batters the dough into rolls.*). Don't argue with me Fred Fincher! The Carraways are coming! Hurrah! Hurrah! One, two. (*She pats up two rolls*). And I'm putting them both in the large bedroom! (*She moves the rolls aside*). And you, Fred Fincher—(*She takes up some dough on her bat*) can like it or lump it!

(*She slaps it down on the table, and breaks into song. Mary looks over the bannisters.*).

MARY. I've taken yours, Mum. (*She exits*).

(*Rose sags, then goes on working mechanically. There is a tap on the door. She starts, then approaches the door fearfully. She opens it. It is* SUNNY, *carrying a large flower-pot.*).

SUNNY. Thanks, my dear. I 'ad my hands full.

ROSE. Oh, do be careful, Grandad. (*She helps him into the room*).

SUNNY. (*Tottering forward on her arm*). That's my gel! If you'll just 'elp me over to the dresser naow.

(*They move to the dresser*).

ROSE. What are you goin' to do, Grandad? I can't do with a plant on my dresser, you know.

SUNNY. Oh, can't you, Rosie? Well, come on over 'ere then. (*They creep across the room together*). What about up on the mantelpiece, eh?

ROSE. All right, Grandad, if you like. Let me put it up. (*She goes to take it*).

SUNNY. No. No. That won't do. Anyone can see that. Too warm up there, I'm thinkin'. Let's try it over there. (*With Rose supporting him he sets off round the room again, trying the pot in various places.*).

ROSE. What about the windowsill, Grandad?

SUNNY. That's a very good idea. Let's try it. (*On they go to the windowsill.* SUNNY *puts the pot on it.*).

ROSE. There! That'll be very nice when it comes up,

SUNNY. Oh, nothin' ain't goin' to come *up*. I 'avn't put anythin' in yet.

ROSE. Oh. Well, if you do plant somethin' it'll take the place of the hydrangea there. (*She points to a sickly plant*).

SUNNY. Mm. 'Tis a bit dog-eared n' it.

ROSE. I'll help you outside with it.

SUNNY. No. No. I don't feel like doin' any more today. I think I'll 'ave a sit down naow.

ROSE. (*Helping him into a chair* D.L.). There we are! Settle down for a while, Grandad, while I get on with the rolls.

SUNNY. Ah! That's better. 'Ad a nice little stroll round, didn't we?

(*Rose returns to her bread*).

ROSE. Chrysanths good this year, Grandad?

SUNNY. Mine are. Other folks' don't look too merry. Nobody don't know nothin' about them round 'ere, 'cept old 'Arry and me. And old 'Arry don't know much.

ROSE. (*Cautiously*). Grandad.

SUNNY. Yes gel? (*Seeing the bats*). 'Ere, what are you usin' there?

ROSE. My old bats for stool-ball.

SUNNY. (*Chuckling*). What an idea! Givin' up the game then?

ROSE. Of course not! We're playin' Coaling Barty this week.

SUNNY. Reckon you'll get an innings this time?

ROSE. Oh, I'm sure to—*this time!*

(*She volleys a piece of dough on to the table.*).

ROSE. (*After a moment*). Grandad.

SUNNY. Yes, gel?

ROSE. Grandad.

SUNNY. I can 'ear you, gel.

ROSE. (*Carefully*). What do you think of the Carraways?

SUNNY. Carraways? Carraways? You mean them East Enders come down 'ere 'oppin' every year?

ROSE. Yes. Do you get on with them?

SUNNY. Well, naow, I used to like old George Carraway. Decent old chap 'e was.

ROSE. What about the others?

SUNNY. Young Alf was a nice sort of lad—clever too. They say 'e's got on.

ROSE. Yes. But Grandad, what about old Mrs. Carraway and her daughter?

SUNNY. (*After a moment's pause*). We-ell, they liven the place up a bit don't they?

ROSE. Yes. I suppose they do.

SUNNY. What are you worryin' about the Carraways for?

ROSE. Oh nothing, Grandad.

SUNNY. Well, somethin' must 'ave made you think on 'em.

ROSE. It isn't anythin'—really Grandad. They just came into my head.

SUNNY. Oh. Can't imagine them comin' into anybody's 'ead—except perhaps with a hatchet! (*He laughs*). 'Course Carraways 'ave been 'oppin' as long as I 'ave, you know.

ROSE. Longer I believe, Grandad.

SUNNY. Oh, I don't know about that.

ROSE. Well, maybe not.

SUNNY. Reckon the most noise in the whole hopgardens comes from round the Carraway's bin. Fred's 'ad some fine old shindigs with them, you know.

ROSE. Yes, I know. (*She looks anxiously out of the window*). Fred's late.

SUNNY. Yes, there's no doubt they're a rare bunch.

ROSE. Yes. Er—don't let's talk about them any more, Grandad.

SUNNY. (*Lost in thought*). My old master used to say, those London pickers do three hundred pounds worth of damage on my farm—and two hundred and ninety-nine pounds of it's done by Carraways.

ROSE. (*Agitated*). Yes, Grandad. Never mind about them now.

(*She has finished the rolls and has set them out on a tray for proving*).

SUNNY. (*Loudly*). 'Carraways'll be the death of me,' 'e used to say when 'e found 'is hedges and stacks all broken down—'Carraways'll be the death o' me!' Don't know as they were though—could've been anybody took the lid off the well!

ROSE. Sh!

SUNNY. What's the matter? Why sh?

ROSE. Fred'll be here in a minute.

SUNNY. Well, what are you gettin' so nervous about?

ROSE. Nervous? Don't be silly, Grandad. I 'aven't got a nerve in my body.

SUNNY. That's right, gel. Take things as they come.

ROSE. (*Moving across the room with the tray of rolls*). Easy-going Rosie, that's me.

FRED. (*Off*). ROSE!

(*Rose gives a jump that sends the rolls flying.*).

ROSE. That's Fred! Oh dear! Oh dear!

SUNNY. Never mind, gel. They 'aven't lost nothin'—they've gained a bit!

(*He helps her pick them up—getting his fingers sticky*).

ROSE. (*Hastily retrieving rolls*). He's early isn't he?

SUNNY. Thought you said 'e was late?

ROSE. Well, he is late—but he's still too early! I mean—Oh, Grandad what are you doin' with that roll! (*She siezes it from him*).

SUNNY. (*Wringing his hands*). You got a dishcloth or something, Rose?

(ROSE *doesn't hear, for just then* FRED *enters.* FRED FINCHER *is in his late forties, with a temperament soured by constant communion with nature. He pauses on the threshold, brooding*).

FRED. (*Darkly*). Reckon there's a frost comin'.

ROSE. Oh gracious!

SUNNY. Don't look like it to me.

FRED. You 'avent' got a cup o' tea goin,' I suppose?

ROSE. Aren't you havin' somethin' to eat?

FRED. No. I can't stop for food this time o' the year.

SUNNY. (*Holding out his hands*). Couldn't I 'ave somethin' to wipe my—

ROSE. Well, just sit down a minute, Fred, anyway. You look tired out.

FRED. No more then usual. (*He sits* C. *and mops his neck*)

SUNNY. Rose, do you think I could— (*He grabs at her apron*).

FRED. (*Regarding rolls*). What's gone wrong with this lot?

ROSE. I dropped them.

FRED. Dropped them! Looks like you've been moppin' the floor with 'em.

SUNNY. Go on, Fred. It's only clean dirt. Rose, would you mind passin' me—

FRED. Am I goin' to get that tea?

ROSE. Yes, Fred.

(SUNNY *abandons hope and begins licking fingers*).

FRED. Today or tomorrow!

ROSE. (*Taking a teapot from the stove*). There's some here hasn't been standin' long, Fred.

(*She pours him a cup*).

FRED. Reckon this weather'll finish the lot of us.

ROSE. I thought you said we needed a dry spell.

FRED. That was when it was rainin' I said that.

ROSE. You want it fine for the hoppin', don't you?

FRED. Oh, there's a week or more to go before we begin that.

ROSE. (*Brightly*). I thought the hops looked very good this year.

FRED. Well, I don't know where you were lookin' then. Things would be a bit different if the old man let me have a free hand, I can tell you. (*He drinks*). Like as not we'd make a bit o' money.

ROSE. The farm does all right, Fred, surely?

FRED. We could do with a whole lot of new machinery. You should see the stuff over at Four Crosses.

ROSE. Well, that's a millionaire's farm, Fred. You said yourself all those fancy appliances come off his income tax.

FRED. Anything new that comes on the market—they've got it. Hop-picking machine—five thousand pounds—and they just bought it like a sack of seed potatoes.

ROSE. (*With a start*). Hop-picking—Oh yes!

FRED. (*Grimacing*). When did you make this tea—last Easter?

ROSE. Well, it won't be long now before we're swarming with people again.

FRED. No.

ROSE. 'Course I know they're a nuisance sometimes, but it all makes for a bit of life, doesn't it?

FRED. They're a downright pest, the lot of them. Still it may not be so bad this year.

ROSE. What makes you say that? (*To* SUNNY). Want some tea, Grandad?

SUNNY. (*Removing his fingers from his mouth*). No thanks. I feel a bit sick.

FRED. What on earth are you doin', Dad? Look at the mess 'e's in, Rose.

ROSE. Oh Dad, why didn't you ask for something to wipe your hands on! I'll get the dishcloth.

(*She crosses to get it*).

ROSE. What made you say the pickers wouldn't trouble you so much this year, Fred?

FRED. (*Smiling grimly*). 'Cause there won't be no Carraways among them.

(ROSE *drops the cloth in alarm.* SUNNY *heaves a sigh and finishes off his hands on a cushion*).

ROSE. (*Apprehensively*). What makes you think that, Fred?

FRED. Old Tom Jevons told me they've been writin' round to all the cottages askin' for a room—if you can imagine it!

SUNNY. What do they suddenly want to stay in a cottage for?

ROSE. The old woman's not well.

FRED. What's that?

ROSE. (*Confused*). I mean I suppose it's because old Mrs. Carraway's gettin' on.

FRED. Yes. Believe it *is* somethin' like that. Anyway, nobody can take 'em—or nobody wants to, more likely.

SUNNY. But they've always 'ad a 'ut before.

FRED. Well, it seems they can't do that any more with the old girl queer.

ROSE. (*Feelingly*). I do think someone ought to have had them.

SUNNY. Well, well, well! So the Carraways aren't comin' this year. Won't seem the same without 'em.

FRED. No. It's the best news I've heard in months.

ROSE. (*Desperately*). Oh, but it does seem a shame for them.

FRED. For *them*? What about us? I can tell you when I heard they weren't comin' down, I felt like a great weight was lifted off my shoulders.

ROSE. But they're such good pickers, Fred.

FRED. Ay. Good at pickin' rows. You wait and see, Rosie, you're goin' to notice a big difference this year.

ROSE. (*Unhappily*). Yes. I don't doubt that.

(MARY *comes downstairs. She has changed her dress*).

MARY. Can I make myself a sandwich, Mum? I'll be in later for supper.

ROSE. All right, dear.

MARY. (*Passing behind* FRED'S *chair and making signals*). Don't forget—you know what!

ROSE. (*Hurriedly*). No, I won't!

MARY. (*Ominously*). I heard a train come in just now.

(*She passes into the scullery*).

FRED. What's all this about trains?

ROSE. Nothing, Fred. Mary heard a train come in.

FRED. Yes? (*He waits*).

ROSE. (*Lamely*). Just now.

FRED. (*Drily*). So what are we supposed to do? Come out in boils?

MARY. (*Off*). Mum's got somethin' to tell you, Dad.

FRED. Oh?

ROSE. It's nothing important, Fred. It'll keep.

FRED. You might as well tell me now I'm sittin' listenin.'

MARY. (*Off*). Yes, go on, Mum.

ROSE. (*With a scowl at the scullery*). Well, Fred—

FRED. Mm?

ROSE. Well, I—

MARY. (*Entering*). Go on, Mum, spit it out. (*She carries ham on a plate and moves to dresser to make sandwich*).

ROSE. I've been thinkin', Fred. We've got quite a lot of room here, haven't we?

FRED. Yes. Reckon we have now.

ROSE. Well, I thought we could take in a paying guest or two. Just for the end of the season, say.

FRED. Can if you like. Managed all right when you did it before, didn't you?

ROSE. Oh yes. It was no bother at all.

FRED. Well, so long as they don't get under my feet it won't trouble me. (*He rises*).

ROSE. Er—Fred—

FRED. Reckon I'll 'ave a sandwich now I've seen it. (*He goes into the scullery*). Go on.

ROSE. (*Calling*). Oh, when you come out will do.

(*She is very agitated*).

SUNNY. (*In a loud whisper*). I know what you've done! You've told the Carraways they can come 'ere, 'aven't you?

(ROSE *leaps up, clapping a hand over his mouth*).

ROSE. Sh! (SUNNY *struggles.* ROSE *lets him go.*)

SUNNY. Cor! You'll catch it!

ROSE. (*To* SUNNY). Dad!

SUNNY. Carraways in this house!

ROSE. Shut up! (SUNNY *is rocking with laughter*).

SUNNY. (*Jerking his thumb towards the scullery*). 'E's goin' to damn near die!

ROSE. (*Hissing*). If you think it's so funny why don't you try tellin' him yourself.

SUNNY. No fears! He's your husband!

ROSE. He's your son!

SUNNY. I've never been too sure about that. He never got that funny-lookin' nose from me. But the baker 'ad one similar! (*He giggles*).

ROSE. Oh Dad!

MARY. Oh, get it over with, Mum, before it's too late.

ROSE. Too late?

MARY. Well, if they're supposed to arrive today.

SUNNY. Today! (*He is overcome with mirth*).

ROSE. (*Bringing rolls to the stove*). Oh, do stop laughing and make room for these rolls.

(FRED *returns with a piece of ham. He regards his father's shaking figure*).

FRED. What's the matter with him? Got warble fly?

ROSE. (*On knees with tray*). Fred, there's another thing I want to—

FRED. (*Take a slice of bread and folding ham in it*). Leave it till I come in tonight, Rose.

(*He moves to the garden door*).

ROSE. But it may be too late by then, Fred.

FRED. Why? What's goin' to happen between now and then, for goodness sake— (*He stops*). 'Allo? Sounds like someone at the gate.

(*The tray drops from* ROSE'S *nerveless fingers on to* SUNNY'S *feet*).

SUNNY. What're you doin', gel? All over my boots!

FRED. Nice tasty rolls we're goin' to have there.

MARY. (*Excitedly at window*). Somebody's coming up the path, Mum!

(*There is a crash outside the door, followed by a series of thuds on the woodwork*).

FRED. Who in hell's that! They'll have the door down in a minute!

(*He flings open the door.* NORMAN BATES *stands on the doorstep. He is about nineteen years old. Usually solemn and self-possessed, but at the moment a trifle dishevelled. He wears a dapper lounge suit.* ROSE, MARY *and* SUNNY *sigh with relief*).

NORMAN. (*Politely*). Good evening.

FRED. (*Roaring*). What in thunder do you think you're doin' makin' all that row? Is anythin' wrong?

NORMAN. Why no, I—

FRED. Then who in the name of heaven do you think you are, creatin' that racket! What's the matter with you! Do you want to knock the house down? Makin' us all jump like that. What do you imagin' you're playin' at, eh?

NORMAN. Nothing. I just tripped over the step and fell against the door.

(MARY *laughs*).

ROSE. (*Recovering herself*). Oh dear. I do hope you haven't hurt yourself.

NORMAN. I'm quite all right, thank you.

ROSE. It is a silly old step. I used to fall over it myself when I first came here.

FRED. (*Sarcastically*). Oh, I'll have it taken away! Then you'll all go flat on your faces goin' out instead of comin' in! What was it you wanted, young fellow?

NORMAN. Well, my name is Norman Bates. I hope you won't think me rude, sir, but I rather hoped I could get some accommodation here.

FRED. (*Mollified*). Well, there's an odd thing. You were just talking about the same idea, weren't you Rose?

ROSE. Er—yes. In a way.

FRED. Come in then. Don't stand there. (NORMAN *enters*). What do you mean by accommodation? A bedroom? (NORMAN *nods*). Well, we've got a big double one would hold four like you, 'aven't we, Rose?

ROSE. (*Anxiously*). Oh no, Fred!

FRED. What do you mean —oh no Fred?

ROSE. I think the little one would be more suitable.

FRED. Why poke him away in there? The big room is much better. Nice and light and airy—and the bed's more comfortable than ours if you ask me.

NORMAN. (*Doubtfully*). It sounds very nice indeed.

FRED. It is. Looks out across the hop gardens. Down 'ere on holiday?

NORMAN. No. I—want to pick hops.

FRED. (*Surveying him*). Oh do you!

ROSE. We haven't started yet.

NORMAN. Oh. Well, I knew it began about this time and I thought I'd come down here anyway and put in a bit of study first.

MARY. Study?

NORMAN. I'm a teacher.

SUNNY. Eh?

MARY. A teacher.

SUNNY. (*Impressed*). A preacher. Mm.

NORMAN. You see I thought this would be an excellent way of getting to know a little more about the agriculture of my own country. You know, one does so much reading and so little observing that one tends to know more about how they grow rice in China than about the crops from our own farmland

FRED. Does one now.

NORMAN. Yes. So I decided it was time to go out and study agricultural methods right in the fields themselves.

FRED. I thought you said you wanted to pick hops.

NORMAN. (*Quickly*). Oh yes, I want to pick them. I'm sure I'll learn more that way too.

ROSE. Well, I think that's very nice.

FRED. (*Regarding* NORMAN'S *appearance disapprovingly*). It's work you know. You can 'ave a go, I suppose, but I don't think you'll care for it.

ROSE. Well, it doesn't matter if he doesn't, Fred. After all it's not the money he's interested in. He's studying.

NORMAN. Er—well. I'm tougher than I look, you know. I'm considered something of a sportsman.

ROSE. Really? I'm interested in sport

NORMAN. Oh yes? (*He ponders*). Which?

ROSE. Stoolball. I play for the village.

NORMAN. Oh yes. That's something like cricket, isn't it?

ROSE. Yes.

FRED. (*Disdainfully*). Except the bats are different and the wickets are different and the balls are different and the rules are different—otherwise they're very similar.

ROSE. We only play a set number of overs, you see.

NORMAN. Oh. But surely that means that sometimes the players don't all get an innings?

ROSE. That's right.

MARY. That's where Mum comes in. She's the player who doesn't get an innings.

ROSE. (*Cheerfully*) Well, someone has to make the tea!

(*They laugh*)

NORMAN. You think you'll be able to take me in then, Mrs.—

ROSE. Fincher. Oh yes. It'll be nice to have you. You must have a talk with my daughter Mary here. She's in the Post Office. She's *supposed* to be studyin' too!

NORMAN. Oh yes. (*He bows to* MARY). How do you do.

ROSE. (*Indicating* SUNNY). And this is Mr. Fincher's father. (NORMAN *nods.*)

SUNNY. Just call me Sunny, lad. By name and nature, you know. (*He half rises and sticks out a hand*).

ROSE. Do mind those rolls by your feet, Dad. They're provin'.

SUNNY. You're right there. Provin' a ruddy nuisance.

(*He sinks back*).

NORMAN. Er—about the terms, Mrs. Fincher.

ROSE. Well now will you want full board?

NORMAN. Yes, please.

FRED. It's four pounds a week, isn't it, Rose?

NORMAN. (*Taken aback*). Oh.

FRED. You won't get in anywhere else. Beautiful room that big one. Take 'im up to see it, Rose.

NORMAN. Oh, I'm sure it's worth it.

FRED. It's worth more! Well, I'm off now. Have you got that pigfood ready, Rose?

ROSE. Not yet, Fred.

FRED. What's the matter with you? I haven't got all day! (*He goes out*).

ROSE. I'll put it out the back in a minute.

SUNNY. (*Calling*). And we 'ope you enjoy it!

(*Pause*).

ROSE. (*To* NORMAN). Would you like to see your room?

NORMAN. Yes, please.

ROSE. } I suppose you wouldn't like the smaller room?
NORMAN } I suppose I couldn't have the smaller room?

(*They both laugh*).

ROSE. I'll do it much cheaper, of course.

NORMAN. I'd much prefer the smaller room.

ROSE. I'm so glad . . . . Because there are already two ladies sleeping in the big one.

NORMAN. Oh. It's just as well then, isn't it?

(*He moves to the stairs*).

ROSE. (*Following him*). You see, Mr. Fincher doesn't know about the two ladies.

NORMAN. (*Puzzled*). He doesn't?

ROSE. I hope you don't mind but you'll have to go through their room to get to the bathroom.

NORMAN. Well, I don't mind—if the ladies don't.

ROSE. Oh, they won't bother—and anyway I don't suppose you'll be going through very often will you?

NORMAN. No. That is—I don't suppose so.

ROSE. I'll make up your bed. (*They go off*).

SUNNY. Looks like we're goin' to 'ave quite a house party afore we're finished. Nice lookin' young man that, eh?

MARY. I can't think what a fellow like that wants with hop-picking. Mum doesn't bother to find out a word about him.

SUNNY. Didn't he say he was an observer or something?

MARY. That's no reason to take away someone's job who may need the money. And anyway who does he think he is. Studying our ways indeed! Makes us sound like a lot of guinea-pigs!

SUNNY. Oh, I don't know naow.

MARY. I think it's a cheek to come making yourself a nuisance when everyone's up to their eyes in work. I can just see what it will be—prying and poking and taking notes and getting in the way of people trying to earn an honest wage.

SUNNY. Never 'eard you talk so nasty about anybody afore, Mary. Taken a likin' to 'im ,'ave you?

MARY. Oh Grandad! (*She flounces away and sits* C.)

SUNNY. Thought you were supposed to be goin' out?

MARY. (*Nonchalantly*). Not especially. I was only goin' to listen to some of Joan's records. (*She glances upstairs*). But I don't suppose she's got any new ones anyway.

SUNNY. Go and get some fresh air, gel. Stuck in that stuffy post office all day.

MARY. No. As a matter of fact, I've got a book from the library I haven't looked at yet. I think I'll stay in and have a read tonight.

SUNNY. Go along with you. You've got plenty of time. The young man'll be with us for a long while yet—Fred willin'.

MARY. (*Rising angrily*). Oh, no-one ever has a minute's peace in this house!

SUNNY. Ah, don't be cross, dear. Your poor old grandad's only teasin'.

MARY. (*At garden door*). Poor old grandad is going to wake up one day with an axe in his head!

(*She goes out, slamming the door*).

SUNNY. (*Chuckling*). Eh, the little pickle!

(NORMAN *comes down the stairs. He sits* L.)

NORMAN. Is it going to be a good season for hops, do you think, sir?

SUNNY. Well, I don't know whether you'd call it good. Promises to be more *interestin'* than usual.

NORMAN. I'm afraid I've come rather early.

SUNNY. You're not the only one. The Carraways are supposed to to be comin' today.

NORMAN. Carraways ?

SUNNY. The ones Rose 'as put in the big room. Old Mrs. Carraway and her daughter.

NORMAN. Oh.

SUNNY. Matter of fact we thought you were them. Rosie nearly jumped out of 'er skin.

NORMAN. She doesn't want them to come ?

SUNNY. No. No. It's Fred. 'E can't stand 'em—and she 'asn't told 'im they're 'ere. Proper fireworks there'll be. (*Chuckling*). You'll be glad you came !

NORMAN. Were they supposed to come by train ? Only there were two women who got out at the station just now.

SUNNY. What did they look like ?

NORMAN. One was rather elderly and the other well—sort of middle-aged.

SUNNY. It could've been them. But what happened to them ?

NORMAN. They got into rather an argument with the ticket collector.

SUNNY. That's them !

(ROSE *comes hurtling down the stairs*).

ROSE. They've come ! They're here ! They've arrived. They're at the gates !

SUNNY. Well, you don't 'ave to worry about tellin' Fred any more.

ROSE. He's never goin' to forgive me for this but I just hadn't the heart to refuse the poor old lady.

(*She opens the door.* MRS. CARRAWAY *and* DOLLY FAGG *enter. The old lady is grim visaged and aggressive,* DOLLY *travel worn but cheerful.* MRS. CARRAWAY *pauses on the threshold and casts a derogatory glance round the room. She gives a sniff that places the whole building beneath contempt*).

MRS. CARRAWAY. I'd sooner 'a bin in the 'ut.

DOLLY. Now then, Ma, don't start as soon as you arrive. How do you do, Mrs. Fincher. It's very kind of you to 'ave us.

MRS. CARRAWAY. (*To* ROSE). I never said I wanted to come 'ere. If it's any inconvenience to you, mate, you can blame 'er. (*She pokes a thumb at her daughter*). She ought to 'ave 'ad children !

DOLLY. (*Ignoring her mother*). It was a real relief to me to find somewhere, I can tell you. What with the doctor darin' me to take Ma 'oppin and 'er darin' me not to. Not that she's likely to pick much. I'll be the one let in for that, I can see.

MRS. CARRAWAY. Oh no you won't. Oh no you won't. The day you can pick as many bushels as I can, my girl, you can consider yourself all right. Just because you was ' Miss Hops ' of nineteen hundred and fried fish. *Miss* Hops ! What sort of a title is that for a decent picker !

DOLLY. Look 'ere, you consider yourself lucky you're down 'ere at all ! (*Turning to* ROSE). 'Ow you been keepin', Mrs. Fincher ?

ROSE. We're all fine, thank you.

DOLLY. (*To* SUNNY). 'Allo Mr. Fincher.

SUNNY. (*Struggling to his feet*). 'Ow do you do!

MRS. CARRAWAY. (*Shaking his hand*). 'Ow do you do. Sit down, mate, before you fall down.

(SUNNY *subsides*).

SUNNY. I understand you 'aven't been well.

MRS. CARRAWAY. I was all right till *they* got at me. Nothin' but fuss, fuss, fuss!

DOLLY. That's not fair, Ma. You 'ad all the care and attention in the world—and if it 'adn't been for that—

MRS. CARRAWAY. I'd a'been better in 'alf the time.

SUNNY. My old pal 'Arry's been 'avin' funny turns lately. It's 'is 'eart.

MRS. CARRAWAY. There's nothin' wrong with my 'eart.

SUNNY. I didn't say there was.

MRS. CARRAWAY. I'm as fit as you any day—*and* me legs 'aven't give way!

SUNNY. (*Firmly*). Nor 'ave mine! Still go on with my gardenin,' I do. Just pottin' up a plant naow. Excuse me. (*He rises and totters out bravely, shaking off* ROSE's *arm*). Leave me alone, woman. Fuss, fuss, fuss! (*He goes out into the garden*).

MRS. CARRAWAY. 'E's beginnin' to look 'is age, you know.

ROSE. Yes. He doesn't get about much these days. As a matter of fact his old pal Harry's passed on—couple of months back. But 'e doesn't know yet and we haven't liked to tell him. They were lads together, you know.

MRS. CARRAWAY. That was a tidy while ago! (*She spots* NORMAN). Who's this? Thought it was a daughter you 'ad.

ROSE. Yes, I have. This is Mr. Bates. He's a hop-picker too.

NORMAN. How do you do.

MRS. CARRAWAY. (*Suspiciously*). He's no 'op-picker.

ROSE. Well, he hasn't done any before, no.

NORMAN. I'm doing it as a sort of experiment. I'm a kind of observer.

MRS. CARRAWAY. Look son, if you're not doin' it for the money, you leave it alone and make room for someone who is.

NORMAN. Well, as a matter of fact I—

MRS. CARRAWAY. World's full of people like you nowadays. Talkin' 'igh class and tryin' to do a workin' man out of a job. What do you do for a livin'?

NORMAN. I'm a teacher. At least I'm going to be.

MRS. CARRAWAY. Teacher! Ph! I've 'ad a basinful of them. Always after my Jimmy they were. Sendin' notes, callin' round, keepin' on and on at 'im. I felt really sorry for the kid. 'E never 'ad a moment's peace. Worry, worry, worry.

NORMAN. But what was all the fuss about?

MRS. CARRAWAY. Well, they wanted 'im to go to school, see?

NORMAN. Oh.

DOLLY. 'E's grown up now, of course.

ROSE. Is 'e comin' down this year?

DOLLY. Only to collect us in 'is car.

MRS. CARRAWAY. Done all right, Jim 'as. Turn 'is 'and to 'anythin'. (*She stabs at* NORMAN). Never 'ampered by an education, that's why!

NORMAN. No. Er—can I take your bag?

MRS. CARRAWAY. (*Grasping it to her*). 'Ere you leave that alone.

NORMAN. I only mean to put it in your room.

DOLLY. Oh, all right. You can take mine too. And the bird cage.

(NORMAN *takes them up*).

MRS. CARRAWAY. Never mind the little one—that's personal! And don't shake that cage about—you'll make the bird sick as a dog!

(NORMAN *carries the luggage upstairs*).

You wait till you see young Jim's Rolls—big as a hearse!

DOLLY. No, Ma, that was last month, it's a pale blue Triumph Dolomite now.

MRS. CARRAWAY. (*Proudly*). What did I say? Turn his hand to anythin' that lad. Make a go of anythin'. Not like this one. (*She thumbs at* DOLLY). Two husbands and both of them threw her out.

DOLLY. I threw them out, you mean! Couple of lazy, loafing—

MRS. CARRAWAY. Not one grandchild to bless me! Not a single one to play round us in the hop-field!

DOLLY. Come off it, Ma. If you'd got them you'd be bashin' hell out of them for gettin' in the way.

MRS. CARRAWAY. Well, where's this room supposed to be that we're sleepin' in?

ROSE. I'll take you up to see it.

MRS. CARRAWAY. Can I smell a cuppa tea?

ROSE. I think Fred had the last of it—but I'll make some more.

DOLLY. How did 'e take to the idea of us comin' 'ere?

ROSE. Oh, he was—he was very pleased.

DOLLY. (*Surprised*). 'E was?

ROSE. Well, not exactly pleased—perhaps that's the wrong word.

MRS. CARRAWAY. What was the word? A rude one I'll bet.

ROSE. To tell the truth, I haven't had a chance to let him know.

DOLLY. You mean you haven't told 'im we're sleepin' under 'is own roof?

ROSE. No. And when he does, I'm afraid—

DOLLY. —he's goin' to raise it! Eh?

(ROSE *nods miserably*).

MRS. CARRAWAY. Well, if 'e think it's any pleasure for us to—

DOLLY. There's a fine thing then!

ROSE. Oh, I know I should have mentioned it before, but what with one thing and another—

DOLLY. Ma being one thing and me the other, I suppose.

ROSE. (*Nodding*). I'm sure everything will be all right. If I can just catch him in the mood. The thing is to avoid a shock.

MRS. CARRAWAY. Don't you refer to me as a shock, young woman.

DOLLY. Oh, shut up, Ma. We've got to 'elp Mrs. Fincher. You ought to be thinkin' 'ow we can straighten things out.

MRS. CARRAWAY. I'll straighten out the whole Fincher family if they're not careful. I'll give them 'shock'.

DOLLY. Listen, Ma, is it Mrs. Fincher's fault if 'er 'usband's an old devil? (*To* ROSE). No offence meant.

MRS. CARRAWAY. You got me down 'ere. I didn't want to come in the first place.

ROSE. I think if you could just keep out of the way until I've spoken to Fred.

MRS. CARRAWAY. What we supposed to do? 'Ide under the mat?

DOLLY. You would go 'oppin!

MRS. CARRAWAY. I've gone 'oppin every year of my life and neither you nor the doctor nor nobody else is stoppin' me. So there!

DOLLY. Well, you're not sleepin' out and that's flat. We'll stay 'ere if it kills us. (*To* ROSE). With due respect.

MRS. CARRAWAY. If you don't get me a cuppa tea soon, I'll 'ave turned me toes up anyway.

ROSE. I'll put the kettle on. Have you had anythin' to eat lately?

MRS. CARRAWAY. Not since breakfast.

DOLLY. Oh Ma! We 'ad a bit of dinner before we come out, and you 'ad a pie on Maidstone Station—only you wouldn't eat it.

MRS. CARRAWAY. It 'ad a button in it.

DOLLY. It was your *own* I tell you!

ROSE. Well, anyway, I'll get you a proper meal. You go up to your room and unpack your things. I'll call you when it's ready. Won't be long—it's all laid for us.

DOLLY. Thanks love. That'll be fine.

ROSE. Your room is just up the top of the stairs and along the passage and up two more stairs. You'll see it—the door's yellow.

(DOLLY *and* MRS. CARRAWAY *move to the stairs.* SUNNY *enters from the garden carrying a pot of Chrysanthemums*).

SUNNY. (*To* MRS. CARRAWAY). Goin' up for a rest?

DOLLY. Come on, Ma, let's get you upstairs.

(*She takes her mother's arm*).

MRS. CARRAWAY. (*Shaking her off*). Leave me be! I'm all right! (*She marches off upstairs but once out of sight she calls*). Dolly!

DOLLY. (*To* ROSE). There you are, you see. The poor old thing can't manage the last few.

MRS. CARRAWAY. (*Poking an irate face over the bannisters*). Oh yes I can! I've forgotten me paper bag.

DOLLY. (*Picking it up*). I'll bring it up, Ma.

(MRS. CARRAWAY'S *visage disappears and* DOLLY *mounts the stairs and exits in her wake*).

SUNNY. She's beginnin' to look her age, you know.

ROSE. Oh dear, I'm afraid I've made a terrible mistake. But I've really never had an awful lot to do with them. I suppose distance lent enchantment.

SUNNY. Must 'ave been a pretty good distance.

ROSE. Maybe they grow on you. I'm sure Fred won't mind so much when I explain how Mrs. Carraway's age is tellin' on her. After all we all have to grow old. (*She sighs*). If only she looked a bit more feeble!

SUNNY. Well, anyway, you might tip me the wink when 'e's comin' in, because I think I'd rather not be 'ere.

ROSE. You're a lot of help.

SUNNY. I'm busy with my bulbs and things. I'll do what I can.

(*He moves to the scullery*).

ROSE. (*Following*). Where are you goin', grandad? I don't want you in there! I'm gettin' supper for the Carraways!

(*She follows him out into the scullery*).

(*After a moment, there is the sound of an argument upstairs and* NORMAN *comes hurrying down.* DOLLY *pursues him half-way and stands shouting at him*).

DOLLY. Huh! Just caught you in time, didn't we! Ought to be ashamed of yourself, a chap like you!

NORMAN. I tell you the lock broke! I was trying to put the things *back into* the case.

DOLLY. That's a good one.

NORMAN. But it's true! You can see it's broken!

DOLLY. There was a perfectly good bit of string round it.

NORMAN. Honestly, Mrs. Fagg, I didn't do it. I'd just got it into the room when it fell apart.

DOLLY. So you were havin' a good old rake over our things.

NORMAN. I was trying to pick them up—they were all over the floor.

DOLLY. (*Calming down*). All right! I'll give you the benefit of the doubt. But don't you let me catch you anywhere near our room again.

NORMAN. Yes, Mrs. Fagg. Oh but—

DOLLY. No 'buts'. You keep out or you've 'ad it. Understand?

NORMAN. Yes.

(DOLLY *retires and* NORMAN *sinks gloomily into a chair* C. *The garden door opens quietly and* MARY *enters. She stands looking at* NORMAN *a moment then moves towards him*).

MARY. I'm surprised at a person like you.

NORMAN. (*Leaping up*). Oh! Excuse me, I didn't see you.

MARY. I said, I'm surprised at a person like you wanting to pick hops.

NORMAN. Why?

MARY. You're not the type.

NORMAN. Well, I'm—I'm going to write a thesis.

MARY. On hop picking?

NORMAN. Yes.

MARY. What for? A lecture or something?

NORMAN. Well, no. Just for my own interest.

MARY. I should think it would be terribly dull.

NORMAN. It's what you make of it, you know.

MARY. Do you like teaching?

NORMAN. Well—I haven't done very much yet.

MARY. I'd be scared to death standing up in front of all those children—aren't you?

NORMAN. Er—no.

MARY. You must be very confident.

NORMAN. It's not exactly that. The fact is I haven't actually taken a class yet. I'm only training. (*He laughs lightly*). I may not even pass the exams.

MARY. (*Disdainfully*). I see.

NORMAN. Oh, I expect I shall! But of course if I don't there are plenty of other things to do. Maybe if I plough this teaching caper, I'll get a job as a reporter. I can type.

MARY. And shorthand?

NORMAN. (*Airily*). Oh, that's not always necessary. Half the stories you read are written before the reporter even gets to the place, you know.

MARY. Really?

NORMAN. Of course. Friend of mine was on a local paper for a while. Used to write his whole article—except for the names and ages—on the bus on his way to the event. He got so good at it in the end that he didn't even go to the places at all.

MARY. And he got on all right?

NORMAN. (*His face clouding*). Well, no. As a matter of fact he got fired.

MARY. I always thought I'd like to be a writer or something.

NORMAN. Don't you like working for the G.P.O.?

MARY. Well, it's only a village post office, you know. It's more like being a shop assistant than a government official.

NORMAN. Why don't you transfer to a town?

MARY. It would mean moving away, and I don't think Mum and Dad would like that.

NORMAN. (*Sighing*). No. The old folks are a problem, aren't they?

MARY. I could get over Mum all right, but Dad's pretty difficult.

NORMAN. So I gather. Mind you, I think I can see his point regarding the Carraways.

MARY. Oh, they're not so bad. Nor is Dad really, but they seem to act on each other like liver salts and water. As soon as they get together—fsh!

NORMAN. I must try to be around when they meet.

MARY. You're not likely to miss it!

NORMAN. Your father seemed quite pleasant to *me*.

MARY. Yes. I can't think why.

NORMAN. Thank you.

MARY. But anything that's likely to bring in a little money has his approval. I suppose that was it.

NORMAN. I see.

MARY. You came down very early, didn't you?

NORMAN. Well, my people are away and I thought I'd potter about, you know. I've never seen anything of this neck of the woods.

MARY. There's not much worth looking at here.

NORMAN. (*With a sidelong glance at her*). Oh, I don't know. I'm not only interested in the scenery.

MARY. (*Blushing*). I suppose I ought to help Mum get supper. (*She moves towards scullery*). There's a film show at the British Legion Hall tomorrow night, but they're not very new films.

NORMAN. What is it ?

MARY. Devil Ranger.

NORMAN. (*Laughing*). Good heavens ! Horse opera ! I might have guessed. No, spare me that !

MARY. (*Bridling*). They're not always bad films—and a lot of people never get into town to the big cinemas.

NORMAN. Oh, I suppose it might be interesting to watch the re-actions of an unsophisticated audience.

MARY. (*Coldly*). Oh very.

NORMAN. Isn't there a decent cinema in Maidstone ?

MARY. Yes, but I don't go very often.

NORMAN. Well, I'll take you—although I expect I'll have seen the films in London myself.

MARY. You needn't bother.

NORMAN. It's no bother—I'd like to. That is if you're keen on films.

MARY. I'm very keen on films.

NORMAN. Then why on earth don't you go more often ?

MARY. It costs such a lot—with the train fare on top.

NORMAN. (*Sobered*). Oh, does it ?

MARY. Well, it's a lot to me. It probably wouldn't seem expensive to you.

NORMAN. (*Gulping*). Oh, no. We must find out what's on and I'll take you one evening.

MARY. (*Haughtily*). I'll see if I have any time free.

NORMAN. (*Realising his mistake*). I didn't mean to be rude about country life, you know. I'm only curious.

(ROSE *is heard calling*).

ROSE. (*Off*). Mary !

MARY. (*Calling*). Yes, Mum ?

ROSE. (*Appearing at door*). Lay the extra places in the dining room, dear.

MARY. All right, Mum. (*She moves to dining room door, then turns back to* NORMAN). I daresay when you make an appearance in the village you'll find you're quite an object of curiosity yourself.

(MARY *exits*).

ROSE. Norman—you don't mind me calling you Norman, do you ? Would you go up and call the Carraways down. I've a bite ready.

NORMAN. I'll do my best, Mrs. Fincher.

ROSE. Oh, go on, lad, they won't eat you—anyway not if you tell them supper's ready !

NORMAN. All right, Mrs. Fincher.

ROSE. Oh, and keep an eye open for Mr. Fincher. If you hear him come in, for goodness sake keep the Carraways upstairs.

NORMAN. I will.

ROSE. Perhaps we'd better just take a look round first.

(NORMAN *looks out of the window,* ROSE *out of the door. She then crosses to the scullery and calls in*).

Dad! Look out the back and see if Fred's about.

SUNNY. (*Off*). Don't see 'im nowhere.

ROSE. (*Calling into dining room*). Any sign of your Father, Mary?

MARY. (*Entering*). No, Mum.

ROSE. All right then. Go and get them, Norman.

NORMAN. Righto! (*He goes upstairs*).

ROSE. Come on Mary. (*They go into scullery*).

(*For a moment the stage is empty, then* FRED *enters from the garden door. He is making an entry in a notebook. He moves down to the dining-room door which is open, glances in, puts his notebook away, rubs his hands down his trousers and enters the dining room, shutting the door behind him. Again the stage is bare for a moment, then* NORMAN *comes creeping down the stairs followed by* DOLLY *and* MRS. CARRAWAY).

MRS. CARRAWAY. What are we supposed to be up to, tiptoeing round the 'ouse like a lot of ruddy fairies?

DOLLY. Sh! Mum, will you keep quiet!

MRS. CARRAWAY. I don't see why we've got to—

DOLLY. You want your supper don't you?

MRS. CARRAWAY. I'm not creepin' round like a—

DOLLY. *You want your supper, don't you?*

MRS. CARRAWAY. 'Course I do.

DOLLY. Well, shut up!

MRS. CARRAWAY. I'm 'alf-starved!

DOLLY. (*Hissing*). So am I. So is 'e (*She points at* NORMAN). So just do as I say!

MRS. CARRAWAY. Like a lot of kids! (*Muttering*). You know your trouble—not 'avin' a family. Wouldn't 'ave 'ad no time for this nonsense.

DOLLY. (*Fiercely*). Will you be *quiet.*

(*They have reached the bottom of the stairs*).

NORMAN. Stay here a minute, Mrs. Fagg. I'll see if the coast's clear.

(ROSE *and* MARY *enter from the scullery*).

ROSE. (*Quietly*). Oh, there you are. Good. We'll just take a look and see if the coast's clear. Take a peep out of the door, Mary.

(MARY *does so.* ROSE *peers from the window*).

SUNNY. (*Entering from scullery*). I think the coast's clear.

MRS. CARRAWAY. So what are we supposed to do? Run up a flag?

ROSE. Come on then.

(*With elaborate caution and fearful glances behind them, the group steal towards the dining room, lead by* ROSE. *As they reach the door, it opens.* FRED *stands there*).

ROSE. Fred! (*There is a pause.* ROSE *gives a high little laugh*). Guess who's here!

FRED. (*Roaring*). What in the name of thunder are those two gorgons doin' in my house!

(*Chaos breaks out and the following dialogue takes place simultaneously*).

ROSE. Fred, please! It's all my fault!

DOLLY. Well, there's a gentlemanly greetin' for you!

MRS. CARRAWAY. *Gorgon*! *Gorgon*! Did 'e say *Gorgon*? That's a cheese, isn't it?

NORMAN. No, it's not a cheese, Mrs. Carraway!

MRS. CARRAWAY. I'll give him call me a cheese!

MARY. Oh, for heaven's sake, Mum, why didn't you tell him?

FRED. Get them out of my house!

ROSE. Fred, they're stayin' here!

FRED. Over my dead body!

ROSE. Fred, I've taken them in!

FRED. Then you can throw them out!

MRS. CARRAWAY. Cheese! I'm not stayin' in this house a minute longer!

DOLLY. But we've nowhere else to go, Ma!

NORMAN. It doesn't mean cheese, Mrs. Carraway.

SUNNY. You'll have to let them stay now, Fred boy.

FRED. Get them out of here or I'll kick them out with my bare hands and the rest of you with them. I'll 'ave no Carraways on these premises!

ROSE. Fred, control yourself!

DOLLY. Ma! Take 'old of yourself!

MRS. CARRAWAY. I'll take 'old of *'im*. I'll knock 'im into Kingdom Come. I'll give 'im Gorgon.

NORMAN. But, Mrs. Carraway, it doesn't mean—

MARY. Oh shut up! You're making it worse!

(*The scene becomes pandemonium with* FRED *restrained by* ROSE, SUNNY *and* MARY, *shaking his fists at* MRS. CARRAWAY *who, fighting like a tiger is being held back by* DOLLY *and* NORMAN. MRS. CARRAWAY *grabs a nearby vase and brandishes it.* NORMAN *wrests it from her and swings it away, accidentally hitting* FRED *on the head.* FRED *falls like stone. There is stunned silence*).

NORMAN. I say, I'm most terribly sorry, Mrs. Fincher.

THE CURTAIN FALLS.

ACT II.

It is later the same evening. The scene is as before. The stage is empty for a moment, then ROSE *enters quietly from the dining room behind her. Suddenly there is a clatter upstairs and* NORMAN *comes hurrying down carrying a tray of used crockery.*)

NORMAN. (*Calling back upstairs*). Well, I'm sorry, Mrs. Fagg. I didn't realise! I apologise, Mrs. Fagg!

DOLLY. (*off*). And next time knock!

ROSE. (*Taking tray*). Thank you for bringing their tray down, Norman. Are you sure you won't have something yourself?

NORMAN. Certain, thank you. I'm really most terribly sorry I hit your husband with that vase.

ROSE. Oh, it's all right. It didn't break.

NORMAN. How is he?

ROSE. Not so bad. Having a rest on the sofa.

NORMAN. It was a complete accident, you know.

ROSE. Of course it was. I saw the whole thing. You were only trying to help, I know.

NORMAN. Yes, but does *he*?

ROSE. Now don't you worry your head about that. He'll forgive and forget the whole thing in a week or two.

NORMAN. Oh. Is—is Mary about, Mrs. Fincher?

ROSE. She was sitting outside the door just now. (*She glances out of the window*). Still is, I believe. (*She goes into scullery*).

(NORMAN *opens the garden door.* MARY *is sitting there. She rises and walks in*).

NORMAN. Oh, please don't let me disturb you. You looked so—so peaceful sitting there in the moonlight. It's such a perfect evening.

MARY. I'm being bitten to death by midges.

(*She moves to dresser and toys with things*).

NORMAN. Can I—can I help you?

MARY. Help me what?

NORMAN. With whatever you're doing.

MARY. I'm not doing anything.

NORMAN. Oh. (*A pause*). I suppose you're fed up because I hit your father?

MARY. (*Hotly*). Well, it wasn't a very gentlemanly thing to do, was it? After all you're a great deal younger than he is.

NORMAN. (*Retorting*). But he's much *bigger*!

MARY. I don't see the point!

NORMAN. Well, neither do I! Anyway it was entirely accidental. I was trying to get the vase away from Mrs. Carraway.

MARY. (*Illogically*). Then what, may I ask, does your size matter?

NORMAN. I don't know what you're getting so upset for, you knew there was likely to be a scene with your father.

MARY. No one has *ever* hit my father before!

NORMAN. Well, it can't have been for want of the inclination! I apologise, Mary! I didn't mean that!

MARY. When he's feeling more himself—he'll probably throw you out of the house.

NORMAN. Nice for me!

MARY. That is if I haven't done it already.

NORMAN. I'm becoming popular round here, aren't I? First the Carraways, now you, and father only waiting till he feels more himself! I mustn't let it go to my head!

MARY. Don't worry—there wouldn't be room!

NORMAN. (*Meekly*). But honestly Mary, you don't believe I meant to hurt your father, do you?

MARY. I didn't see what happened.

NORMAN. *Well*, then! It was the vase, you see. I was hanging on to it and old Mrs. Carraway let go suddenly. I went flying and your father was right behind me and just happened to get in the way.

MARY. So that's how it was.

NORMAN. That's exactly how it happened.

MARY. (*Softening and moving in*). Well, if it really wasn't your fault, Norman—

(MRS. CARRAWAY *comes down the stairs, assisted by* DOLLY, *who carries a roll of wallpaper*).

MRS. CARRAWAY. Stop it! (*She brushes off* DOLLY'S *hand*). Don't keep fussing all round me, gel. Buzz off! (*She sees* NORMAN *and approaches him smiling*). Congratulations, young man!

NORMAN. (*Apprehensively*). Congratulations?

MRS. CARRAWAY. On the fight. Never saw nobody laid out neater. You've got an uppercut there like a sledge-'ammer mate. Woomf! You did 'im a treat!

MARY. (*Furiously*). Oh!

(*She rushes out of the garden door just as* SUNNY *is entering*).

SUNNY. 'Ere, mind where you're—

(NORMAN *also rushes past him pursuing* MARY).

—going! Huh! Where's the fire? Ah well, it's the call o' nature, I suppose.

MRS. CARRAWAY. Is it? Well they can keep all that farmyard stuff to themselves, while I'm 'ere.

DOLLY. 'Ow's Mr. Fincher's 'ead?

SUNNY. Not so dusty. Take more'n that to finish Fred.

MRS. CARRAWAY. More's the pity.

DOLLY. Now, Ma, you know what I said. (*To* SUNNY). I've been 'avin' quite a talk to Ma upstairs, Mr. Fincher.

MRS. CARRAWAY. Readin' me a lecture, you mean.

DOLLY. Well, I think we've got to make a proper effort to get along with Fred Fincher. I can see there's faults on both sides all right. I know Ma and me 'ave got our tempers.

MRS. CARRAWAY. You speak for yourself.

DOLLY. But I've made Ma promise not to say one single word unless it's absolutely polite and nice.

MRS. CARRAWAY. I speak as I find.

DOLLY. Well, that's exactly what you're not to do! I don't care what Fred Fincher says to you!

MRS. CARRAWAY. Doesn't need to say anythin' 'alf the time. It's 'is eyes—baleful!

DOLLY. But you've got to try and make yourself pleasant. We've got to forget what's gone before and get to like each other. After all it's only a matter of knowing one another better.

MRS. CARRAWAY. Baleful! Like a couple of cockles!

DOLLY. Now listen Ma, you gave your word.

MRS. CARRAWAY. All right, all right, all right! Don't worry about me. I'll treat 'im like a long-lost son.

DOLLY. Oh Ma! (*To* SUNNY). When young Ernie came 'ome from abroad she threw the flat-iron at 'im. (*To* MRS. CARRAWAY). I said you've got to be nice to 'im.

MRS. CARRAWAY. You don't 'ave to learn me me manners, Dolly. Wasn't so long ago I was tryin' to teach you what a 'ankerchief was for.

DOLLY. Well, you might 'ave tried givin' me one! Now look, are you goin' to do it or aren't you?

MRS. CARRAWAY. I'll do it. But be it on your own 'ead.

SUNNY. Well, that'll make a change from Fred's anyway.

DOLLY. If 'e talks to us at all, Ma, we'll just keep on some safe subject—like the weather.

SUNNY. You don't know much about farmers, do you?

DOLLY. I'll go and tell Mrs. Fincher what we're proposin' to do. She said she'd try and persuade 'er Fred to do the same. A sort of peace pact, you know. Like the foreign countries 'ave with each other.

MRS. CARRAWAY. Yes. Just before they declare war.

DOLLY. (*Gently*). Do me a favour will you, Ma? Everythin'll be all right, we'll be able to stay 'ere in peace, you'll be able to pick all the 'ops you like, get all the fresh air you need and go 'ome feelin' fine; we'll 'ave a nice change from the cookin' and make enough for that winter coat you're after—if you'll just keep your *big trap shut*!

(*She goes into the kitchen*).

MRS. CARRAWAY. That's the manners of today for you! Rude! Disrespectful! They're all the same.

SUNNY. Ay. The young folks are a problem.

MRS. CARRAWAY. 'Course, you know 'er trouble?

SUNNY. (*Dubiously*). Er—no?

MRS. CARRAWAY. No children.

SUNNY. She wanted them?

MRS. CARRAWAY. No, she didn't want 'em.

SUNNY. You mean they'd 'ave sweetened 'er nature?

MRS. CARRAWAY. Well, no. No-one can say children do that!

SUNNY. *What* then?

MRS. CARRAWAY. They'd 'ave served 'er right!

SUNNY. Oh.

MRS. CARRAWAY. I don't 'old with women not 'avin' children. They get above themselves. Got it too easy by far. She tried to stop me comin' down, you know.

SUNNY. Would 'ave seemed a bit queer down 'ere if you 'adn't, I must say.

MRS. CARRAWAY. Bin down every year of me life, I 'ave, and me mother was born in this 'op garden; did you know that?

SUNNY. Was she though?

MRS. CARRAWAY. Don't change much. It's us that changes. I knew the old days was over when there was no more kids comin' down with us, and my Ernie said 'e'd sooner go and pick grapes over in France! My life! Trouble is the youngsters don't need the money like we used to—nor the 'oliday. You won't be pickin' this year will you?

SUNNY. (*Bridling*). Oh, I don't know 'bout that. I'll be goin' down if my old pal 'Arry does.

MRS. CARRAWAY. (*Thoughtfully*). 'Arry, oh yes.

SUNNY. 'Ad a rare set-to last year. First 'e was goin', then 'e wasn't. Said 'e'd go if I did.

MRS. CARRAWAY. And 'e went in the end?

SUNNY. Yes. So o' course I 'ad to. 'E shouldn't 'ave done it. It weren't good for a man of 'is age. It damn near killed me!

MRS. CARRAWAY. Feelin' all right now?

SUNNY. Oh yes, right as rain. It's keepin' workin' does it. Got more to manage 'ere than 'Arry 'as. Nice bit of ground 'e's got there though. Next door to the Manor House, old Mrs. Turner's place—wonderful garden *she's* got. Rare one for propogation 'Arry is. Boasts 'e never bought a plant in 'is life. Mother Nature will provide, 'e always says.

MRS. CARRAWAY. And I suppose she does.

SUNNY. Not 'alf so often as Mother Turner does—did she but know it!

MRS. CARRAWAY. I used to be interested in gardenin'. 'Ad a window box once, but nothin' ever grew in it.

SUNNY. Maybe there was somethin' wrong with your drainage. Or the soil was sour, or of course, you might 'ave underwatered or even overwatered.

MRS. CARRAWAY. (*Thoughtfully*). No, no I think it was because I never set anythin'.

SUNNY. Oh.

MRS. CARRAWAY. Your Fred doesn't improve with keepin', does 'e?

SUNNY. Oh, 'e's not so bad. 'As a lot of responsibility, 'as Fred. Got a lot to manage 'ere.

MRS. CARRAWAY. Don't the owner give 'im a 'and?

SUNNY. Mr. Methews? No. Never gave anythin' much—'cept damn silly orders. Mind you, the old chap's pretty well in 'is dotage—

that's 'alf of it.

MRS. CARRAWAY. The old folks are a problem all right!

SUNNY. So you see why Fred gets niggly.

MRS. CARRAWAY. Not with us, I don't. We only come to 'elp, after all.

SUNNY. Oh, Fred realises that. First one to say what good pickers you are.

MRS. CARRAWAY. I should 'ope so! Anyway, I've given me word of honour I won't start a quarrel, and I'm not goin' to. But Dolly don't trust me.

SUNNY. She's afraid Fred'll make your resolution waver.

MRS. CARRAWAY. Cheeky devil!

(FRED'S *voice is heard outside*).

SUNNY. That's Fred now.

MRS. CARRAWAY. Oh, well, come on, let's go out in the garden while I've still got me honour!

SUNNY. Righto! Follow me!

(*He moves a few steps to the door and sags.* MRS. CARRAWAY *grabs him and hurries him out*).

MRS. CARRAWAY. Mind if I follow in front?

(*They exit into the garden.* FRED *and* ROSE *enter from the dining room*).

ROSE. Fred, for goodness sake, you're acting like a bear with a sore head.

FRED. Well, I've got a sore head!

ROSE. Oh dear, does it hurt very much?

FRED. It's goin' off.

ROSE. Young Norman's terribly upset about it.

FRED. It wasn't his fault. I saw the whole thing.

ROSE. Well, what a pity you didn't dodge!

FRED. Whatever possessed you to let those Carraways into this house?

ROSE. Now Fred, I know I should have talked it over with you first, but I knew it would lead to a row.

FRED. Springin' them on me like that!

ROSE. (*Unhappily*). That was a mistake too! I didn't know you were there!

FRED. Well, there's one mistake I'll put right straight away. We'll put those women back on a train to Tufnell Park.

ROSE. Bethnal Green, dear. But I asked them to come, Fred.

FRED. And I *didn't* ask them to come—I don't want them to stay—and I'm tellin' them to go. Is that clear?

ROSE. Yes, Fred. But I've been talking to Dolly Fagg and—

FRED. I don't care what you've said to Dolly Fagg or what Dolly Fagg's said to you. They're going! Both of them!

ROSE. But poor old Mrs. Carraway—

FRED. She's going first!

ROSE. Fred, be reasonable!

FRED. Reasonable! If there is a family who are never here ten minutes without being in some sort of trouble, who are forever making some kind of complaint, who I never speak to without having a first class argument, whose very name sends goose pimples up my spine—it's the Carraways! And you want me to take them into my home! Don't you realise what it means?

ROSE. Yes I do. It means we'll all have to exercise a great deal of self control.

FRED. I tell you I'm havin' them out of here if it's the last thing I do! Whose house is this anyway?

ROSE. Mr. Methews, Fred. And honestly it's going to make all sorts of trouble if the Carraways take it into their heads to go and see him.

FRED. He'll be pretty wild if they do.

ROSE. He will. He'll be wild with you for letting him get bothered.

FRED. They won't go to Methews.

ROSE. They well might! And anyway, what do you think people will say. Lettin' them come all this way, then turnin' them out of the house?

FRED. Yes. You've certainly made us look pretty daft!

ROSE. Well, we don't have to Fred. Not if we just let them stay. Where's the harm?

FRED. No! No! *No*! I'll be out of my mind in a week.

ROSE. 'Course you won't. You'd be used to them ages before that.

FRED. I won't do it!

ROSE. We'll *have* to, dear. It's an irritation I know, but a man with a strong will like you won't be affected by people like that for long.

FRED. (*Weakening*). 'Ave you thought what life will be like with those two 'arpies all over the place?

ROSE. I've talked it over with Dolly Fagg and we've both agreed on a way out.

FRED. I'll show 'er the way out!

ROSE. They realise that there are certain differences between you, but they're going to undertake not to mention the past nor get on any touchy subjects while they're under this roof.

FRED. Goin' to be very chatty, aren't they!

ROSE. No really, Fred, they've given me their word that they'll say absolutely nothing at all except in the way of pleasantness. Now what about you?

FRED. What *about* me?

ROSE. If you promise to do the same we can't possibly have any rows, can we?

FRED. Those Carraways could quarrel with a blade of grass because it was green.

ROSE. Won't you try it, Fred?

FRED. It's not *me* makes the trouble.

ROSE. I know, dear, but please be extra specially nice—even if you don't feel like it.

FRED. Well, I suppose if they must stay 'ere we'll 'ave to find some way of puttin' up with each other.

ROSE. That's right. After all it's only for a week or so, then they'll be out pickin' all the time.

FRED. Now wait a minute, I never said they were goin' to pick hops.

ROSE. But, Fred, that's why they've come.

FRED. You said they'd come for the sake of the old woman's health. All right. I've agreed to them stayin' here. I'll be out most of the time and when I'm in I'll agree to keep the peace. But I'll not have 'em pullin' no bines—and that's flat!

ROSE. But Fred—

FRED. Not another word! You know very well if they set foot in those hop fields I'll be up to my eyes in trouble with them.

ROSE. Well, let me break it to them gently then, Fred.

FRED. You're always doin' that, Rose—and it nearly always leads to a riot.

ROSE. They'll be so disappointed—at least old Mrs. Carraway will be. Couldn't you let 'er pick *something*!

FRED. Ay. She can stay right 'ere and pick 'er teeth!

ROSE. Oh, you are hard, Fred. You know she hasn't got any worth speakin' of!

FRED. Well, I'll leave 'er mine!

ROSE. Fred!

FRED. Just stop it will you! You've got your way, now give me a minute's peace.

ROSE. (*After a moment*). And you'll keep your temper?

FRED. You wouldn't like me to kiss their hands?

ROSE. Now there's no need to go to extremes, Fred.

FRED. No. We've already done that lettin' them stay! Oh, don't worry. I'll be sweetness itself. They'll be bowled over!

(MRS. CARRAWAY'S *voice off*).

ROSE. Well, you'd better be prepared for your first 'over'—Mrs. Carraway's just comin' in now!

FRED. (*Dubiously*). Oh. (ROSE *moves to the scullery*). Where are you goin'?

ROSE. Now you gave your word, Fred! I must get on.

FRED. But Rose—

ROSE. I'm all behind. What with this and that and nothing but slow music on the wireless all the day.

(ROSE *goes into the scullery.* FRED *prepares to depart, but before he can escape* DOLLY *enters, leading* MRS. CARRAWAY. *They enter from the garden, sheltering under an umbrella*).

DOLLY. Come indoors, Ma! I thought you were havin' your rest!

MRS. CARRAWAY. I've 'ad it. Such as it was!

DOLLY. You'll put yourself back in bed—goin' out without a coat on in the rain!

MRS. CARRAWAY. I was in the shed, I tell you! (*The two women see* FRED). Oh!

(*For a moment there is a heavy silence, then* MRS. CARRAWAY *sweeps forward*).

MRS. CARRAWAY. (*Aggressively*). Now then Fred Fincher!

DOLLY. (*Warningly*). Ma!

MRS. CARRAWAY. (*Checking herself and assuming a regal manner*). How do you do. (*She extends her hand*).

FRED. (*Not to be outdone*). How do you do!

(*He shakes her hand.* MRS. CARRAWAY *withdraws it and shakes off the contamination.* FRED *withdrawing his, wipes it on his trousers with a shudder*).

DOLLY. (*Carefully*). It's so nice to be down in the country again. So beautiful this time of year, isn't it, Ma?

MRS. CARRAWAY. 'Aven't seen anythin' of it yet!

DOLLY. Ma!

MRS. CARRAWAY. All right! All right! (*She sits* D.L.) Tell me, Mr. Fincher what are the 'arvest prospects this year?

FRED. Things aren't so bad so far, Mrs. Carraway. (*Sits* C.)

MRS. CARRAWAY. That's nice. And 'ow are the 'ops keepin?

FRED. (*Ominously*). All right at the moment, Mrs. Carraway.

MRS. CARRAWAY. So kind of you to let us stay 'ere.

FRED. (*With an effort*). It's a pleasure.

DOLLY. Such a nice room that big back one. (*Sits* L.)

FRED. Glad you like it.

DOLLY. Looks like a lovely bed.

FRED. It's the best one in the 'ouse, if you ask me.

MRS. CARRAWAY. Yes. It seemed ever so soft when I 'ad a bounce on it.

FRED. (*Hotly*). 'Ere! Don't you go bouncin' on—(ROSE'S *voice is heard off calling:* "Fred!"). It's a very good bed.

DOLLY. Oh, I'm sure Ma and I'll do very nicely on it. Better than ours at 'ome.

MRS. CARRAWAY. Give it a chance, Doll. That's 'ad a fair bit of knockin' about one way and the other.

DOLLY. We've got ourselves all unpacked, Mr. Fincher. Would you like a roll of paper?

FRED. Well I don't know—I suppose—

DOLLY. I told Ma it wouldn't be necessary but she insisted on bringing it just the same.

FRED. Well, I daresay it'll come in useful.

MRS. CARRAWAY. It's a lovely design—little orange flowers on a beige ground.

FRED. Oh, *wall*paper!

(DOLLY *hands him the roll*).

DOLLY. Of course! Ma always papered the 'ut fresh every year, you know, and I couldn't get 'er to realise we weren't usin' it this time.

MRS. CARRAWAY. It don't seem right.

DOLLY. Anyway, you'd better take it, Mr Fincher, or—who knows—Ma might take it into 'er 'ead to do over the bedroom upstairs.

(*She laughs.* FRED *winces*).

That little girl of yours is growin' up, Mr. Fincher.

FRED. (*Heavily*). I'd want to know a thing or two if she was doin' anythin' else.

DOLLY. (*Brightly*). Pretty little thing too, don't you think so, Ma?

MRS. CARRAWAY. Reminds me of my young sister Edie.

DOLLY. But Edie's dark, Ma.

MRS. CARRAWAY. Oh yes. I don't mean looks so much, but 'er ways, you know. 'Er character. Edie used to come 'oppin.

FRED. (*Bitterly*). I remember 'er. Got 'erself strung up on a pole.

MRS. CARRAWAY. That's right. Same year as Ernie 'ad some little trouble or other with a tractor.

FRED. 'E drove it into the river!

DOLLY. Young scamp! 'E got soaked through!

FRED. They're not comin' down this year?

MRS. CARRAWAY. No. They've emigrated to Australia.

FRED. (*Brightening*). Oh.

DOLLY. It was awful sayin' goodbye to them. Had a terrible time packin' up and tryin' to sell stuff—and you never can, you know! We were always fond of them. It was dreadful seein' them go.

MRS. CARRAWAY. They're comin' back Christmas.

(FRED'S *face falls*).

DOLLY. I expect they'll be goin' up north to live.

FRED. (*Pleased*). Ah!

DOLLY. Mind you, I reckon they'll come down 'ere for the 'oppin just the same—to see us.

FRED. Oh.

MRS. CARRAWAY. And you needn't say it like that. Don't think I didn't 'ear your tone of voice. You won't get better pickers, you know.

FRED. I won't get better wreckers, you mean.

DOLLY. (*With control*). Now I'm not goin' to argue, Mr. Fincher, but that's a very provocative remark.

FRED. Well, I'm not arguin' either but there's no disputin' the fact that there's never a year passed as long as I remember without me 'avin' to see you about some damn thing or other.

DOLLY. That's your business. If you always choose to come pickin' on us. Mind you, I'm not quarrellin' about it now.

FRED. Pickin' on you! Now I don't want no disagreements, but do you mind tellin' me who else I was supposed to go to other than the people to blame?

DOLLY. You know we wasn't always to blame! It's just become a 'abit with you. Something gone wrong!—all right, see the Carraways about it first.

FRED. It's a very good habit. It saves time! Besides I've got so that I can smell the sort of trouble you get yourselves into. I've developed a nose for it.

MRS. CARRAWAY. Well, you might 'ave developed a nicer-lookin' one.

DOLLY. Ma!

MRS. CARRAWAY. Well, 'e's sittin' there insultin' us, isn't 'e?

DOLLY. Not at all. Mr. F ncher and I are merely 'avin' a friendly discussion.

FRED. That's right.

DOLLY. Not that I'm lettin' 'im get away with the nonsense 'e's talkin'.

FRED. Don't tell me I don't know my job. I've managed this farm for Mr. Methews for fifteen years. Fifteen hop seasons I've seen 'ere, and never a year without a catastrophe—and always traced back to a Carraway!

DOLLY. Never!

FRED. (*Firmly*). Sometimes two catastrophies!

MRS. CARRAWAY. That was when we was really tryin'.

FRED. I'm not an unreasonable man, but year after year—apples stolen, gates left open, cattle strayin', hedges broken, rubbish thrown about—

DOLLY. Well, where were we supposed to throw it?

FRED. I don't know. Just don't throw it! Tractors tinkered with, carthorses galloped, wagons borrowed, straw stolen, potatoes pilfered—

MRS. CARRAWAY. (*Cheerfully*). Swedes swiped!

FRED. Bins battered, fences wrecked, stacks fired—

DOLLY. Oh no! Now that I won't 'ave. No Carraway ever set fire to a haystack. We know more about the country than to do that.

FRED. Stacks fired, I say!

DOLLY. Far be it for me to tell you your own business, but you 'ad that stack too near the railway line, if you ask me.

FRED. I'm not askin' you!

DOLLY. Well, I'm tellin' you!

FRED. I know where to build a stack.

DOLLY. Oh yes! Right on top of the railway line, with all the sparks flyin' all over the place. Very sensible!

FRED. I've 'ad stacks there before!

DOLLY. Not that near!

FRED. You can't tell me who sent that stack up. You were seen there—the lot of you!

DOLLY. We was beatin' it out, you big clod!

FRED. That's what *you* say, but you've got enough crimes laid at your door to make it very difficult to believe you didn't 'ave a 'and in that fire. I know what *I* think—no matter what anyone else says. And I know I'm right—so I'm not enterin' into any arguments.

DOLLY. I wasn't arguin'!

FRED. Good.

DOLLY. Just statin' a fact.

(*They relapse into a strained silence*).

MRS. CARRAWAY. (*In a loud whisper to* DOLLY). 'Asn't 'e got somethin' 'e ought to be doin'? I always thought farmers worked so 'ard.

FRED. (*Stiffly*). So they do. You can't rush round doin' what we do. You've got to take it steady so as to keep goin' indefinitely.

DOLLY. They 'ave to save themselves, Ma.

MRS. CARRAWAY. What for?

DOLLY. Posterity!

FRED. Let me tell you I've got a pile of returns to fill in that'll take me half the night!

DOLLY. Doesn't the owner do that?

FRED. Precious few. So I'll trouble you for a little peace and quiet while I'm at it.

DOLLY. Give us a chance! We 'aven't said a word yet.

MRS. CARRAWAY. We'll 'ave sabotaged this year's 'ops next, you see!

FRED. Oh-ho, no! That's something you're not doin'.

MRS. CARRAWAY. Eh?

FRED. Ever since I thought you weren't comin' I've been lookin' forward to this season without a care in the world.

DOLLY. But we are comin'—we're 'ere!

FRED. Well, you'll pull no bines on this farm!

MRS. CARRAWAY. What's 'e talkin' about?

FRED. I've told Rose you can stay 'ere for a bit if you want, but as far as workin' in the hop gardens is concerned—it's out!

DOLLY. But that's all we came down for! Don't imagine it was for the sight of you, do you?

FRED. I don't care. I'm standin' firm.

DOLLY. You can't do that! We've always come! You're not gettin' away with this, my friend.

FRED. (*With finality*). I tell you, I'm not havin' you—nor your mother—nor your export reject of a family down 'ere ever again. Is that clear?

MRS. CARRAWAY. (*Rising*). Where's me umbrella?

DOLLY. (*Firmly*). We're not leavin' Ma.

MRS. CARRAWAY. Who said anythin' about leavin'? I'm goin' to poke his eye out!

DOLLY. We'll see who 'as the last word on this!

FRED. Yes, and it'll be me!

DOLLY. Don't you be so sure!

MRS. CARRAWAY. Stand back, Dolly. Stand back. Let me get at him!

DOLLY. You keep out of it, Ma. Do you want another attack?

MRS. CARRAWAY. I 'aven't 'ad me first one yet—out of the way!

(*She dives at* FRED, *with her umbrella. He counters with the roll of wallpaper. They fence a little.* ROSE *runs in from the kitchen.* MARY *and* NORMAN *from the garden.* MARY *and* ROSE *join the fray.* NORMAN *moves out of range* D.R.)

(MRS. CARRAWAY *sinks into* L. *chair after a sharp prod from* FRED. *He stands back panting*).

ROSE. (*To Dolly*). This is a fine way to keep the peace!

DOLLY. He started it!

ROSE. You promised!

DOLLY. I defy a saint to put up with him.

ROSE. *I* do!

DOLLY. Then you're a fool.

MARY. Don't you call my Mother a fool!

FRED. You keep out of this, Mary.

ROSE. You gave me your word, Fred, and I expected you to keep it.

FRED. Then you're a fool!

MARY. Don't you call my Mother a fool!

ROSE. You keep out of this Mary!

FRED. I told you what would happen.

ROSE. Why did you have to stay in here talkin'? Just askin' for trouble. Look at that poor old woman! (*She indicates* MRS. CARRAWAY). You may have seriously injured her!

(FRED *looks a bit anxious.* MRS. CARRAWAY *lies back, eyes closed*).

Get along with you, you great ox. You've done enough harm here!

FRED. This is my house. I'll go when I please.

ROSE. You'll go straight away!

FRED. (*Hotly*). Who says I will!

ROSE. Mr. Methews; he wants you over at the big house right away.

FRED. Oh. Oh, that's different. (*He moves to the door, then turns*). But let me tell you, you brought this on yourself, Rose. And as for the Carraway family, if they lay one hand on a single 'op, I'll take a shotgun to them!

(*He goes out. There is a pause*).

DOLLY. I'm sorry, Mrs. Fincher.

MRS. CARRAWAY. (*Opening her eyes*). I'm not!

ROSE. Oh, Mrs. Carraway, are you all right? I really don't know what to say.

MRS. CARRAWAY. Then you 'aven't got no imagination. I know what to say, I—

DOLLY. No, Ma, please! You've said enough! Besides, young Mary's 'ere.

MARY. I hope Dad didn't hurt you, Mrs. Carraway. (*She turns to* NORMAN). Why didn't you do something, instead of just 'observing' us!

NORMAN. Well, last time I tried to help I only made things worse. Besides, it seemed pretty well matched.

MARY. Well, I hope you're getting lots of useful information on rural activity!

(SUNNY *enters from the garden*).

SUNNY. Mr. Methews is askin' for Fred.

ROSE. I know. He's gone over.

SUNNY. (*Looking round*). Did I miss somethin'?

ROSE. Oh, Dad, Fred's absolutely determined not to let Mrs. Carraway and Mrs. Fagg work. (*Sits* C.)

SUNNY. What? Not now they're stoppin' 'ere? (*Sits* D.L.)

ROSE. No. He says they can stay here but he doesn't want them in the fields.

SUNNY. Ah dear! He can be very unreasonable at times, can Fred.

MARY. I think he's just perverse.

NORMAN. Well, the situation is a sort of challenge to him, isn't it?

As he sees it, he's given in over them staying and any further retreat on his part would seem like weakness. It's a perfectly natural reaction in a man of his nature. It's a well-known physychological fact that has to do with a kind of inverted inferiority complex and—er—and—er—that kind of thing.

(*He trails off, aware of a roomful of cold eyes fixed on him*).

MARY. Have you got any constructive suggestions, Mr. Bates?

NORMAN. Er—no.

MARY. Well, I've got one for you—go and boil your head!

ROSE. Mary, dear!

NORMAN. What did *I* do? (*He appeals to* ROSE). Tell me that—what did *I* do?

DOLLY. Just don't butt in on a family row, Sunny Jim.

(NORMAN *exits into the dining room*).

SUNNY. You know, I can't really understand Fred's attitude—when you think how much we've got in common—you and us. We've got the same approach to life, you might say. The same—er—

MARY. Philosophy.

SUNNY. That's it. The same physopholy. An age-old creed to live by, you'd call it, as we've shared since time began. Townsmen like you and countrymen like us—always driven by the same ancient force—

MRS. CARRAWAY. To do the other feller in the eye!

SUNNY. That's right.

DOLLY. After all, you've got to outwit the next one or you find yourself overboard.

MRS. CARRAWAY. Mm. But it's a hard fight when a family starts runnin' low on wits!

(*She casts a baleful stare at* DOLLY).

DOLLY. Now don't blame me for all this! We're only wishin' Fred Fincher would realise we're all in the same boat and we ought to pull together.

MRS. CARRAWAY. Oh, throw a lifebelt at 'er somebody!

DOLLY. Now listen Ma, I've got you all the way down 'ere, after goodness knows what song and dance, and nobody's goin' to stop us workin' now we're 'ere. Come to that, we've got to earn the fare back!

MRS. CARRAWAY. Jim's takin' us by car.

DOLLY. Not till after the 'oppin. 'E's up north for the next three weeks.

ROSE. Well, if it comes to that you can stay here till he can collect you.

DOLLY. That's all right by us if you don't mind not bein' paid.

ROSE. Oh dear. Well, I don't know whether—

MARY. That's one way of getting round Dad. Tell him he's going to have to give you free board and lodgings!

ROSE. Oh, he'd never hear of us doing such a thing!

DOLLY. Then he'll have to pay our fare home.

MARY. I'd like to see him do that!

SUNNY. I reckon you've got 'im! Don't see what else he can do but let you work.

DOLLY. 'E'll be glad in the end, you know.

ROSE. Oh yes. We really need experienced people like you.

SUNNY. Well, it looks as if it'll be all right after all.

ROSE. (*Worried*). I'm not so sure. You know Fred! Supposin' he just won't give in, like Mr. Bates says.

DOLLY (*Grimly*). He'll be sorry if he doesn't! The devil finds work for idle hands!

MRS. CARRAWAY. (*Leering*). And we can give *him* a few tips!

ROSE. (*Anxiously*). I certainly hope Fred will see reason!

SUNNY. He will! He's got no choice!

(*Everyone brightens up*).

ROSE. I think the financial side of it will be the deciding factor for Fred, all right. Ph! I must say it'll be a relief. I can't say I enjoy being a sort of buffer state.

MARY. Well, you do *ask* for things, Mum.

ROSE. I always try to please everybody.

MARY. That's the point. You can't possibly please *everybody*.

DOLLY. It's her kind heart, bless her. The trouble with really good people is, they expect everyone else to be the same.

ROSE. It was really myself I was thinkin' of, you know. I wanted to have you here to stay. It's so nice havin' someone different to talk to for a change, and to have somethin' goin' on.

SUNNY. Don't see why you aren't satisfied with Fred. You've got him goin' on pretty well all the time.

DOLLY. I should think you get bored stiff sometimes livin' in a little place like this. I would.

ROSE. I don't know about bored. Haven't got much time for that. I've got a couple of hundred chicken, you know.

DOLLY. I meant in the amusement line.

ROSE. Well, of course, I've got my stoolball.

MRS. CARRAWAY. You've got your what?

ROSE. I play stool-ball for the village, every Saturday afternoon and some evenings. We've got a match tomorrow.

DOLLY. I'd like to see it—if you're playin'.

ROSE. Well, I'll be in the team, but very often the game's over before I get a chance to bat.

DOLLY. That doesn't sound fair to me.

MARY. I know. I've told her she ought to kick up a fuss about it. She never says a word!

ROSE. Well, I really am going to mention it if it happens again tomorrow. After all, why shouldn't I bat?

MRS. CARRAWAY. Because you're probably no good.

DOLLY. Ma!

ROSE. Oh but she's right—I'm not—but nor is anyone else! This village holds the record. In eight years we've never won a game!

MARY. So that's no excuse for them!

MRS. CARRAWAY. Well, you'd better try some of this chlorophyl toothpaste stuff—maybe you've got myxamatosis. Can I smell a cup of tea ?

DOLLY. Oh really Ma ! Don't worry, Mrs. Fincher, I'll make 'er one. I brought down a little primus stove. It leaks a bit but it'll do for the odd cup up in the bedroom and—

ROSE. (*Hastily*). Oh, you don't need to do that, Mrs. Fagg. I'll make tea any time you fancy it. I'm an old teapot myself.

(*She rises*).

DOLLY. Well, I'll give 'and.

(*She follows* ROSE *into kitchen*).

MRS. CARRAWAY. Well, that's a drink of some sort comin'. Sooner 'ave 'ad a Guiness, but beggars can't be choosers, can they ?

SUNNY. My old pal 'Arry likes Guiness, but not me. You can't see what's in it, I reckon.

MRS. CARRAWAY. What do you expect to see in it—a crocodile ?

SUNNY. You never know. My old pal 'Arry 'once 'ad a barmaid's earring in 'is.

MRS. CARRAWAY. Drop or stud ?

SUNNY. Nearly choked to death. Mind you 'e laughed it off.

MRS. CARRAWAY. (*Thoughtfully*). Let's see now—'Arry—'e's the one you 'aven't seen lately, isn't 'e ?

SUNNY. That's right. My fault really. 'Aven't been out much. Expect 'e's off doin' some o' them recordin's for the wireless. What they call folk-music and such. You know, old songs 'anded down by ear.

MRS. CARRAWAY. What do they want to record them for ?

SUNNY. Don't ask me. But they was very keen. Nobody knew any except 'Arry. Mind you I'm not sayin' 'e didn't sing 'em nice—'e didn't as a matter of fact, sung 'em awful—but *I'd* never 'eard 'em before and nor 'ad anybody else round 'ere.

(*There is a pause.* MARY *moves with elaborate disinterest towards the dining room. At last she reaches the door and cautiously glances back to make sure she is unobserved.* SUNNY *and* MRS. CARRAWAY *are sitting together heads archly on side, drinking in her actions. With a snort she marches into the dining room and slams the door*).

SUNNY. Gone to make up with 'im.

MRS. CARRAWAY. More fool 'er. Always let 'em come to you, that's the way. Never 'ad no nonsense from Mr. Carraway, I didn't. It's the man's place to apologise.

SUNNY. Even when 'e's in the right ?

MRS. CARRAWAY. 'E never was in the right. It stands to reason a woman's got more common sense. She 'as to deal with the essentials of life, feeding and clothing, birth and death and so on. Mind you, that doesn't apply to Dolly. If ever there was an exception to the rule— ! You know 'er trouble ?

SUNNY. (*Tentatively*). No children ?

MRS CARRAWAY. Seven strappin' kids, that's what she needed. Like I 'ad. Ah, a family 'as a wonderful effect on a woman. (SUNNY *regards her doubtfully*). The rough and tumble of the little ones round the place, the comings and goings, the excitement, the things they get up to, the Christmasses, the Fireworks nights, the birthday parties! Ah! And the blessed relief when they marry and move out.

SUNNY. I remember Mr. Carraway. Got on very well we did.

MRS. CARRAWAY. Yes. Not unlike 'im in looks, you aren't neither. Good lookin' man 'e was. In a repulsive sort of way. 'Course, drink was 'is downfall.

SUNNY. Yes. I can remember the year 'e fell in the combined 'arvester. Fred was very cut up.

MRS. CARRAWAY. *Fred* was! (*She laughs*). Oh, Carraway was always a clumsy devil. One thing, doesn't look as if drink'll be our downfall. I could just go a Guiness.

SUNNY. Wouldn't mind a pint myself.

MRS. CARRAWAY. Well, there's no risk of it—I haven't a bean.

SUNNY. (*Feeling in his pocket*). Wonder what I've got. Maybe I could raise enough for both of us.

MRS. CARRAWAY. Pity your legs are so bad. We might nip down the corner.

SUNNY. I can nip as well as the next one. Just let's have a bit of a scout round . . . . .

(*He moves round the room feeling in jugs, vases etc.* MRS. CARRAWAY *helps*).

MRS. CARRAWAY. (*Looking in a jar*). 'ere, what's this?

(*She turns the jar over and out fall some coins*).

SUNNY. (*Excitedly holding up a jug*). Here's some more!

MRS. CARRAWAY. (*Looking in jug*). You'd better get your glasses on—it's milk bottle tops! (SUNNY *collects the coins from the jar*). 'Ave you got enough? Can you borrow some?

SUNNY. (*Counting*). Who from? Rose hasn't got none—and Fred! Might as well try and get manure from a rockin' 'orse. Wait a minute, I reckon there's enough. Let's go before Rose comes back.

(*He giggles*).

MRS. CARRAWAY. Come on then.

(*They move to the door.* MRS. CARRAWAY *opens it and* SUNNY *makes his halting way out*).

SUNNY. I've got to watch this step.

MRS. CARRAWAY. Get a move on, or Dolly'll be in. She'll do 'er nut!

(*Laughing fearfully they exit, closing the door softly behind them.* MARY *enters from the dining room, followed by* NORMAN).

MARY. I was sure I heard the door go. I thought it was Dad.

NORMAN. You know I think you all take the wrong attitude towards your father. You should be grateful that he is a bit different and not just like everyone else.

MARY. I don't see why?

NORMAN. Too many of us today are turned out of the same mould.

We're not 'characters' and our fathers and mothers aren't 'characters', but our grandfathers and grandmothers now, they were real individuals. I've never met anyone yet whose grandfather wasn't extraordinary in some way.

MARY. Mine isn't.

NORMAN. (*Slightly irritated*). Well, yours is alive! But you've got an unusual father instead.

MARY. I don't think he's very unusual. He's just bad tempered.

NORMAN. (*Solemnly*). There's probably something organically wrong with him.

MARY. (*Bridling*). I think that's very rude! He's probably bad tempered because people are so infuriating!

NORMAN. (*Appealing*). Please, Mary, don't be cross.

(*He waits meekly while* MARY *simmers down*).

MARY. (*At last*). Would you like to hear some records?

NORMAN. Yes, I would. What have you got?

(MARY *opens the gramophone and begins to take out records*).

MARY. I expect you'll *know* them all, or perhaps they're not your taste.

(NORMAN *joins her and reads out the labels*).

NORMAN. (*Delighted*). George Shearing! But he's terrific!

MARY. (*Happily*). Yes, isn't he!

NORMAN. (*Reading*). Ertha Kitt! Wonderful! 'Small Talk!'

MARY. (*Excitedly*). There are some classical records too!

NORMAN. (*Taking one*). King Christian! You've got some of my favourite records, Mary!

MARY. I've got Romeo and Juliet—the sound track!

NORMAN. Oh good! Let's play some.

MARY. (*Shyly*). Which part?

NORMAN. The fighting of course!

MARY. Oh. (MARY *puts it on at the appropriate place*). My girl-friend has lots more.

NORMAN. Has she? I'd like to meet her!

MARY. (*Jealously*). Well, I'll *see* if I can arrange it.

NORMAN. Isn't it good that we like the same sort of music, Mary. When can we have a real session?

MARY. Oh, any time, I expect. Perhaps we—

NORMAN. Sh! Do you mind if I turn up this bit?

MARY. No.

(NORMAN *turns it on loudly and conducts it energetically.* MARY, *laughing, joins in the spirit of the moment by taking up an imaginary cymbal. The noises bring* ROSE *and* DOLLY *hurrying on.* NORMAN *turns towards them, his imaginary baton flaying the air. Automatically, the women take up 'instruments'*—DOLLY *the violin and* ROSE *the bagpipes! a choice that deters* NORMAN *only momentarily. The fight music comes to an end.* NORMAN *switches it off and takes a bow*).

NORMAN. That will be all for this afternoon, gentlemen.

(*They are all laughing*).

ROSE. I'll get that tea!

DOLLY. 'Ere, where's Ma?

ROSE. And Dad?

MARY. I think they must have gone into the garden.

DOLLY. Oh, isn't that just like Ma. With no coat on, I bet.

ROSE. They'll both catch their death of cold!

(*They open the garden door and call*).

DOLLY. Ma! Are you there?

ROSE. Dad! Where are you?

(*They give back as the two old folk appear, arm-in-arm and carrying a bottle each*).

MRS. CARRAWAY. We just popped out to the pub.

SUNNY. Well, we didn't actually get there. We met young Johnny Wheeler—

MRS. CARRAWAY. And Sunny's legs being collapsible we sent the kid down.

SUNNY. So we're goin' to 'ave one 'ere instead. (*Sits* D.L.)

MRS. CARRAWAY. Anybody want a drop?

SUNNY. Lets 'ave a few tumblers, Rose.

ROSE. Eggcups, you mean.

DOLLY. Where did you get the money from, Ma?

MRS. CARRAWAY. Mr. Fincher paid.

ROSE. Where did *you* get it, Dad? (*She moves quickly to the jar and looks inside*). I see!

SUNNY. (*Rather shamefaced*). I—I hope you weren't savin' it for something special, Rose.

ROSE. No. I don't mind a bit.

SUNNY. Oh, that's good.

ROSE. It was *Fred's* money.

SUNNY. Oh lor!

(*After a moment's troubled pause,* SUNNY *begins to chuckle and everyone joins in. They are all laughing hilariously, when the garden door opens.* FRED *stands there. Silence falls*).

ROSE. Well! There you are, Fred!

(FRED *enters. Others part before him. He seats himself* C. *Mary and Norman move* U.L.)

FRED. (*Evenly*). Seems to be a lot o' noise goin' on in 'ere.

ROSE. We were just havin' a laugh, you know, Fred.

DOLLY. Have a drink with us, Mr. Fincher?

FRED. A drink? What 'ave you got?

DOLLY. Guiness.

FRED. That'll do me.

(*He smiles enigmatically.* DOLLY *and* ROSE *exchange pleased glances.* DOLLY *wrests the bottle from* MRS. CARRAWAY *and pours it into a glass brought by* ROSE).

ROSE. Mrs. Fagg and Mrs. Carraway and Mr. Bates have been makin' themselves at home, Fred.

FRED. Oh. (*He drinks*).

ROSE. We've been havin' some music.

FRED. Oh. Nice. (*He smiles again. Not a pleasant sight*).

ROSE. You seem very pleased, dear. Did Mr. Methews have something interesting to say?

FRED. He did. (*He drains glass*).

ROSE. (*Vaguely*). Oh good.

MRS. CARRAWAY. (*Boldly*). Now about this 'op pickin', Mr. Fincher,—(ROSE *and* DOLLY *silence her.* ROSE *with a gesture,* DOLLY *by clapping a hand over her mouth, which the old lady bites savagely*).

ROSE. Will you have another, Fred? There's some ale here somewhere.

FRED. Mm. Why not?

(ROSE *searches for* SUNNY'S *bottle, finding it inside his coat. She pours it*).

ROSE. I know you prefer this.

FRED. Where's all this come from?

SUNNY. (*Defensively*). It was Mrs. Carraway's idea.

ROSE. Yes. Wasn't it nice of her? (*She crosses her fingers*). Because you were kind enough to let them stay here.

FRED. (*Noncommittally*). Mm.

ROSE. I told them they didn't need to bother.

FRED. It's up to them—it's their money.

(SUNNY *winces*).

DOLLY. I said it was the least we could do as you were lettin' us stay 'ere for nothin'.

FRED. I wasn't aware I was doin' any such thing.

DOLLY. Well, *we* 'aven't got any money to pay for board and lodging. We were relyin' on earnin' it down 'ere.

FRED. Were you now.

DOLLY. Otherwise you'll 'ave to keep us for free.

FRED. Will I then?

DOLLY. Or else pay our fares 'ome.

FRED. You got yourselves down 'ere—you get yourselves back.

ROSE. Fred dear, you'll have to let them work.

SUNNY. I don't see what else you can do, Fred lad.

MARY. There's no other way, Dad.

NORMAN. Looks like you'll have to give in, Mr. Fincher.

FRED. (*Quietly*). They'll pull no bines on this farm.

MRS. CARRAWAY. Oh indeed! We'll see about this! You're not the owner! We'll see Mr. Methews himself. We'll see whose goin' to pick 'ops—

FRED. (*Rising and thundering*). You'll do no pickin' because there'll be no pickin'!

ROSE. Fred!

FRED. And that goes for the lot of you!

NORMAN. What do you mean, Mr. Fincher?

ROSE. Fred, he's not—

FRED. (*Nodding*). They're goin' to be picked mechanically. Mr. Methews is sendin' them over to the machine at Four Crosses.

SUNNY. That's a bit sudden, isn't it ?

FRED. It is. Left it to the last minute to tell me too.

DOLLY. The machine !

FRED. They've bought one on the next farm. You can see it from 'ere. It's big enough.

NORMAN. You mean they won't want any helpers, Mr. Fincher ?

FRED. That's right. But don't you worry, you'll be able to watch them being picked just the same.

NORMAN. (*Anxiously*). But I wanted to work.

DOLLY. (*Angrily*). They can't do that ! He should 'ave let us know !

FRED. Mr. Methews can do anythin' he likes.

MRS. CARRAWAY. What's all this about ?

DOLLY. They're usin' a mechanical picker, Ma.

MRS. CARRAWAY. What's that ?

DOLLY. Oh, you've 'eard of them.

MRS. CARRAWAY. (*Stubbornly*). No, I 'aven't.

DOLLY. Don't talk nonsense. Everybody was on about them last year. (*To* FRED). But they don't pick clean, Mr. Fincher. You know that.

FRED. Yes, they do.

NORMAN. But won't you need anyone at all ?

FRED. I've got all the hands I need right here on the farm. The machine'll do the rest.

(*He sits at his desk* L.)

MRS. CARRAWAY. Machine ! Who ever 'eard of a machine pickin' 'ops.

MARY. Haven't you seen one, Mrs. Carraway ? They're wonderful !

SUNNY. They're that all right ! Dozens of little steel fingers goin' like this !

(*He demonstrates, flipping his fingers up and down*).

MRS. CARRAWAY. It can't do it ! I don't care how many fingers it's got goin' like this !

(*She flips her fingers*).

DOLLY. Oh, Ma, they've been usin' them for ages. It's just that I never imagined them gettin' one 'ere.

ROSE. Oh, we never would have. They're five or six thousand pounds. We couldn't afford that.

MRS. CARRAWAY. There you are ! I knew they weren't goin' to use no machine. It's just that Fred Fincher tryin' to put us off. (*Sits* C.)

DOLLY. No, Ma. He's not.

MRS. CARRAWAY. Don't you believe it, gel.

DOLLY. Ma, they're takin' the bines over to another farm.

MRS. CARRAWAY. I'm not 'avin' nobody do me out of my job.

DOLLY. It's not a case of someone else, Ma.

MRS. CARRAWAY. They needn't think I'll let a lot of chavvies and diddygoys push me out—

DOLLY. (*Exasperated*). There won't be no pickers at all, Ma. Don't you understand ?

MRS. CARRAWAY. You can't tell me Mrs. 'Arris and that crowd won't be down just the same. And what about the gypsies? How are they goin' to earn a bit for the winter?

DOLLY. I don't know, Ma, but you'll 'ave to face the fact that we're not wanted any more.

MRS. CARRAWAY. Why not? Tell me that!

DOLLY. Oh Ma! (*Gently*). Maybe we can go to some other farm.

MRS. CARRAWAY. I'll do no such thing! I've come down 'ere every year of my life and my mother and her mother before her. I'll pick on this farm or not at all. You give in too easy, Dolly. They need us as much as we need them.

DOLLY. Not any more, Ma. It's mechanised.

MRS. CARRAWAY. Mechanised! Lot of flippin' fingers flippin' up up and down. Lot of 'ops that's goin' to pick.

DOLLY. (*Wearily*). I think you'd better go up to bed, Ma. You look tired. We'll talk about it tomorrow.

MRS. CARRAWAY. There's nothing to talk about. (*She rises*). I'm goin' to pick 'ops and that's that!

DOLLY. (*Crossly*). Then you'll probably find yourself carried up the conveyor belt and dropped in the machinery!

MRS. CARRAWAY. (*At stairs*). And the beer would taste the better for it!

(*She stalks off upstairs*).

DOLLY. (*Sitting* C.) Oh gawd!

ROSE. Mary, go and get out some extra blankets for Mrs. Carraway. I'll take her up that cup of tea she wanted so much. I'm afraid she doesn't seem to have understood the position, Mrs. Fagg.

(*She goes into the kitchen.* MARY *runs upstairs*).

MARY. (*On stairs, to* NORMAN). Will you stay on just the same?

NORMAN. No. I—I don't think so.

MARY. (*Disappointed*). Oh. (*She disappears*).

(*There is a pause.* FRED *is busy with his books*).

SUNNY. Well, at least there won't be no argument as to whether old 'Arry's goin' to work or not this year. That'll be a relief.

FRED. 'Arry? Why? (*Remembering*). Oh no!

SUNNY. (*To* DOLLY). Reckon you'll 'ave a 'ard job convincin' the old girl. Stubborn 'nt she?

DOLLY. She just doesn't want to believe it, that's why. But when she does face up, she'll find it's worse than she thinks.

SUNNY. Why?

DOLLY. Because we 'aven't got the fare 'ome, of course! I must 'ave needed my brains testin' to bring 'er down in the first place.

SUNNY. Well, you'll 'ave to get 'ome, won't you? Couldn't you borrow some money?

DOLLY. I've got to get some from somewhere. (*Tentatively*). Mr. Fincher, do you think—

FRED. I never lend money. Surest way of losing a friend.

DOLLY. Well, you don't 'ave to worry about that in this case, do you?

(FRED *ignores this*).

SUNNY. I'd let you 'ave some if I 'ad any, Mrs. Fagg, but I'm blessed if I 'ave!

FRED. There's a shilling or two in the jar on the dresser—you're welcome to that!

(*He carries on with his work*).

DOLLY. Thank you. (*She moves to the jar*).

SUNNY. (*Rising*). Oh, I've just rembered something I wanted to do!

(*He moves hastily upstage to signal to* DOLLY, *behind* FRED'S *back, that the money went on the beer.* DOLLY *comprehends*).

FRED. (*Not looking up*). Can you find it?

DOLLY. (*Holding the jar upside down ruefully*). Yes, thank you, Mr. Fincher.

(DOLLY *sits again rather dejectedly on table*).

NORMAN. What'll you do, Mrs. Fagg? (*Sits* C.)

DOLLY. Oh—somethin'll turn up. Maybe we can hitch-hike.

NORMAN. But you can't do that with Mrs. Carraway.

DOLLY. I don't know.. She'd probably be very good at it. Lie down in the road or something.

(SUNNY *sees all is well and seats himself with a sigh* D.L.)

NORMAN. How much do you need, Mrs. Fagg?

DOLLY. (*Eagerly*). About a quid would do it! Would you mind?

NORMAN. A pound! Well, the fact is—frankly, Mrs, Fagg, I was relying on this job as much as you. I—

DOLLY. But I thought you were a teacher just down 'ere to study.

NORMAN. Well, I am interested in it, but it was really for the money I came. You see, I'm still training and I haven't a private allowance and—well—a pound!

DOLLY. I understand, love. Never mind. You are in the same boat, after all. Honest, I don't think I've ever met anybody who wasn't!

NORMAN. It's not that I don't think I'll get it back.

DOLLY. Well, you probably wouldn't.

NORMAN. It's just that— (*He hesitates then takes the plunge*). Oh look, you've got to get home somehow. I can let you have it.

DOLLY. You can?

NORMAN. (*Fumbling in his wallet*). Yes, it'll just give me enough to settle with Mrs. Fincher and get back home myself.

DOLLY. You are a good boy.

NORMAN. (*Handing her the pound*). I was saving it for something, but it's not so important as you getting the old lady back to London.

DOLLY. (*Moved*). Look 'ere, lad, tell you what I'll do. (*She removes her brooch*). I'll give you this brooch as security. It's worth three pounds. I know that for sure! There!

NORMAN. (*Taking it*). Oh but—

DOLLY. I know I won't get round to sending your pound back, so it's the only safe way.

NORMAN. Well, I'll bring it back to you in London.

DOLLY. I know you will and you hang on to it till I give you your pound. And don't go giving it to Ma!

NORMAN. I won't!

ROSE. (*Entering with tea and biscuits on tray*). Here's yours, Mrs. Fagg.

DOLLY. I'll 'ave it upstairs with Ma, thanks. Goodnight all!

(*They murmur in reply*).

ROSE. I'll come and see you all settled for the night.

(*She goes up the stairs*).

DOLLY. (*To* NORMAN, *indicating* ROSE). She'll 'ave to 'ave the eternity ring Mr. Fagg gave me the night before we broke up!

(*She goes upstairs*).

NORMAN. (*Rising*). I suppose there's absolutely no job around the place that I could do, Mr. Fincher?

FRED. (*Looking him up and down*). I'm afraid there's nothin' *you* could manage.

NORMAN. I see.

FRED. Better go back to the city with the others.

NORMAN. I thought farms were short of workers.

FRED. Of *skilled* workers, lad. I've no chance this time of year to be teaching a newcomer.

NORMAN. What about all these forms and returns you have to do? Couldn't I do those for you?

FRED. Son, it's taken me fifteen years to find out how to do them myself. Don't reckon I could explain them to anyone else this side of Christmas.

NORMAN. I see. Well. That's that.

FRED. That's that. (*He returns to his work*).

NORMAN. I think I'll go up to bed. Goodnight.

SUNNY. Goodnight, lad. (*Norman moves slowly upstairs*).

FRED. (*Not looking up*). Don't you want something to drink?

NORMAN. No, thank you.

(MARY *comes down the stairs, meeting* NORMAN).

MARY. (*Shyly*). Cheer up! Stay over tomorrow and I'll come to the pictures with you in Maidstone, like you said.

NORMAN. (*Abashed*). Oh, well, I don't think—I mean, we can't do that now. You see, I—I have to get back to London.

MARY. (*Humiliated*). Oh, of course, if you'd rather not. (*Sarcastically*). I suppose there isn't much point if you're going away!

NORMAN. I'm sorry, Mary. Perhaps there'll be another chance. I'll come down again.

MARY. (*Lightly*). Oh yes! If I have an evening to waste some time. Goodnight!

NORMAN. Goodnight!

(NORMAN *goes miserably upstairs*).

(MARY *flounces into the room and flings herself onto the rug downstage and propped on her elbows, sulkily plucks a tuft or two*).

(*After a moment* ROSE *comes down and sits* C. *with a sigh*).

ROSE. Old Mrs. Carraway's dusting her sunhat.

FRED. Well, they'll all be gone tomorrow and that'll be the end of it.

ROSE. Yes. I suppose it's worked out for the best.

MARY. (*Fiercely*). I hope you won't go letting any more rooms, Mum. It justs upsets everything.

SUNNY. Ay. Never a minute's peace with all these people turning the place into a circus—even if you do get a bit of a laugh.

FRED. Well, you've no need to worry any more. Tomorrow we'll be rid of them and the whole place will be back to normal. (*He pauses*). So everything's fine.

ROSE. (*After another pause*). That's right.

(*Pause*).

SUNNY. Yes.

(*Pause*).

MARY. (*Sighing gustily*). Hm.

(*The Finchers are sunk in abject gloom. They gaze into space.* FRED *looks round at them all. Walks up to the stairs, turns and glares at them. Strides back to the Centre, looks as if he is about to speak, but instead he sinks down into a chair and is looking more depressed than anyone else as—*

THE CURTAIN FALLS).

ACT III.

It is midday the next day. The scene is the same, but an ironing board now stands L. ROSE *is ironing her white shorts for the stoolball match. After a moment* FRED *enters from the garden. He looks round the room.*

FRED. Well?

ROSE. No, they haven't yet, Fred.

FRED. Oh.

ROSE. Your dinner's on the stove, Fred. I've had mine.

(FRED *takes his plate from the stove and carries it to the table, then gets himself a knife and fork*).

FRED. Stoolball?

ROSE. We're playing Coaling Barty. We've been just waitin' to get them over here to pay them back for that cracked kneecap Daisy Morley got and for those Kit-e-Kat sandwiches they dished up!

FRED. (*Eating*). I thought the season was over.

ROSE. It's just a friendly match.

FRED. Sounds like it. (*He eats in silence for a moment*). Why haven't they gone?

ROSE. I—I didn't want to send them off without a meal inside them, Fred.

FRED. You said that breakfast-time. I suppose you'll still be shovelling food into them at teatime?

ROSE. No, they're catchin' the two-thirty. It's the best after the ten-thirty.

FRED. Why didn't they catch the ten-thirty?

ROSE. Well, they were all packed up and ready and when we looked round to see if they were all there—old Mrs. Carraway wasn't.

FRED. She never has been!

ROSE. She was out all the morning.

FRED. 'As she come back yet?

ROSE. (*Indicating dining room*). Just finishing her dinner. Looks tired though and a bit peculiar. It's been a shock for her, you know Fred.

FRED. (*Not unkindly*). Dolly oughtn't to let the old girl go wanderin' across the fields at her age.

ROSE. *Was* she over the fields?

FRED. Yes. I caught sight of 'er over Four Crosses way.

ROSE. (*Unhappily*). Having a last look round the farm, I suppose. Poor old thing.

FRED. Slipped over she did, but she didn't seem to bother none.

ROSE. She's wonderful for her years, you know.

FRED. Where's Sunny?

ROSE. He said he was goin' to lift a few onions for me.

FRED. He's not out in the garden now.

ROSE. He's upset that old Mrs. Carraway's leavin', They've taken to each other, I think, bein' of an age. You know I sometimes suspect he knows old Harry's passed on. You really ought to tell him, Fred.

FRED. Why me?

ROSE. Well, I'm sure it's goin' to upset him and I couldn't bear to do it. Poor old man.

FRED. Well, 'Arry was gettin' on—'e knows that. We've all got to go sometime. 'E'll be poppin' off himself before long.

ROSE. That's what I mean, Fred. You could put it so much better than I could.

(ROSE *holds up the shorts*).

FRED. I wish you wouldn't wear those things, Rose. You don't suit them.

ROSE. But we all wear them.

FRED. I know. Like a lot of laundry bags. There's—there's too much of them!

ROSE. Fred Fincher! Last week you said there was too much of me, so I've let them down especially!

FRED. Well, there's something wrong with them!

ROSE. There is *now,* yes. I can't get the pleats right. I wish I hadn't touched them at all.

(DOLLY *and* MRS. CARRAWAY *enter* D.R., *arguing*).

MRS. CARRAWAY. All right! All right! All right! So I've lost it!

DOLLY. Oh really, Ma! (*To* ROSE). I've got all our things piled up ready to leave and now Ma's umbrella's missin'.

MRS. CARRAWAY. You don't 'ave to worry. It's *my* umbrella. Nobody's askin' you to buy another one—

DOLLY. (*Ignoring her*). Have you seen it, Mrs. Fincher. (ROSE *shakes her head*). Did you take it out with you this morning, Ma?

MRS. CARRAWAY. I don't know—I—

DOLLY. You did take it, I saw you—

MRS. CARRAWAY. Well, what are you askin' me for?

DOLLY. And it wasn't even rainin'. I suppose you've dropped it in some ditch or other.

MRS. CARRAWAY. Very likely.

DOLLY. There's no point in my goin' out to look. It might be anywhere. Honest, for two pins—! I paid a lot for that umbrella.

MRS. CARRAWAY. But you gave it to *me.* Didn't you?

DOLLY. That's not the —

MRS. CARRAWAY. (*Persisting*). It's *mine*—isn't it?

DOLLY. But—

MRS. CARRAWAY. It's *mine.* Is it *mine*?

DOLLY. Yes, and it's probably gone down a ditch—

MRS. CARRAWAY. All right! I don't care if it's gone down a drain! (*To* ROSE). Fuss! Fuss! Fuss! You know 'er trouble? Never 'ad nothin' really worth fussin' over. Ought to 'ave 'ad kids—or corns!

DOLLY. Ma 'asn't got the first idea what things cost nowadays.

MRS. CARRAWAY. Why should I? I'm not goin' to buy anythin'.

DOLLY. You said that well!

MRS. CARRAWAY. That's right! Call me mean. Go on!

DOLLY. (*Obliging*). You're mean! And the only reason I overlook it is because you 'aven't got any money! (*She turns to* ROSE). What are you supposed to be doin' with that? (*She indicates ironing*).

ROSE. It's for the match this afternoon, but I'm havin' trouble with the pleats.

DOLLY. Trouble! You're doin' them all wrong. What time's that train go?

FRED. Two-thirty.

DOLLY. Well, give it 'ere. Let's 'ave a go for you. I wasn't in the laundry for nothin'.

ROSE. Were you?

DOLLY. (*Nodding*). Hand finisher for seven years—except during the war, of course, when I was unpicking the initialled handkerchiefs. (*She begins ironing*). You've got them all facing the wrong way.

ROSE. Oh.

DOLLY. They'll lie flatter like this.

FRED. I knew she'd done something damn silly with it.

MRS. CARRAWAY. Where's Sunny?

ROSE. He's lifting some onions.

MRS. CARRAWAY. Well, that's one way of gettin' 'em. (*Sits* D.L.)

(FRED *gives an unexpected laugh*).

ROSE. (*To* DOLLY). It is good of you, Mrs. Fagg.

DOLLY. Dead easy when you know how, love. If we were stayin' on, I'd show you some tricks of the trade.

MRS. CARRAWAY. Well, you'll 'ave to wait till next year.

DOLLY. (*With a despairing gesture*). Next year!

MRS. CARRAWAY. They'll need human beings again, my gel. You'll see, this new-fangled machine's just a flash in the pan.

DOLLY. Like the 'orseless carriage!

ROSE. I'm afraid it had to come, Mrs. Carraway.

FRED. It's the pickers themselves have been the trouble. Get a bit of bad weather and you're never sure of havin' enough of 'em.

MRS. CARRAWAY. Rain never damped down a Carraway.

ROSE. That's true. You must admit that, Fred.

FRED. I know that.

DOLLY. And there's been times when you've been glad of us. What about our young nephew Alfie and that killer dog? You wouldn't 'ave 'ad many sheep left, would you?

FRED. Mm. I'll grant you that. Always beat me 'ow the kid 'ad the nerve.

DOLLY. Dogs always fascinated young Alfie.

MRS. CARRAWAY. And 'is father before 'im. White City ought to 'ave paid 'is widow a pension.

DOLLY. And who was it kept on to you till you put up a first-aid 'ut like the other 'op gardens?—a Carraway!

FRED. And who was the first casualty ?—a Carraway ! Hadn't had the bandages in there a day and he uses them all up !

DOLLY. Well, it justified puttin' it up, didn't it ?

ROSE. Everyone was ever so pleased with you, Fred.

FRED. Hm.

ROSE. And I can remember that time when Mrs. Fagg's little niece relieved you of Mr. Methews all through the hoppin'.

DOLLY. Oh yes. Little Beattie Carraway. Do you remember, Ma ? We were keepin'the kid in our 'ut to quarantine 'er and old Mr. Methews went round them—lookin' into livin' conditions as 'e called it. Poor child—she tried to keep 'im out. " What's the matter with you ? " 'e says. " Measles, want a spot ? " she says. And he thinks she's bein' cheeky and comes in and goes off at 'er. Next thing, he's gone down with it 'imself for the rest of the season.

ROSE. If that wasn't a good turn, Fred, I don't know what is.

FRED. It did keep 'im from under my feet for once, I'll say that.

MRS. CARRAWAY. And do you remember the year the bines caught fire ? It was a Carraway put it out remember.

DOLLY. Oh shut up, Ma ! It was a Carraway who set light to it !

MRS. CARRAWAY. He only lit the fire where 'e was told. You won't deny that, Mr. Fincher.

ROSE. Did he, Fred ?

FRED. (*Grudgingly*). The wind changed. Oh, there've been faults on both sides, I suppose.

ROSE. (*Amazed*). Well !

MRS. CARRAWAY. Ah, there've been all sorts and conditions of Carraways come down. Good ones, not so good ones—

FRED. And downright bloody ones !

MRS. CARRAWAY. (*Slowly*). They've been born 'ere and they've died 'ere. Swept away down the river one lot were when it flooded bad —along of twenty-five others. All buried together down in the village churchyard. That was a long time ago now. But nobody can't say we're not part of this place. Nobody can't say we've got no right to come down 'ere.

DOLLY. (*Reasonably*). You can't stop changes 'appenin', Ma. It's natural. Nothin's done the same way for ever—someone always finds a better method—

MRS. CARRAWAY. Better !

DOLLY. (*Gently*). Well, a *different* way of doin' things. The time comes for a new order and nothin'll stop it 'appenin' because it comes when it's needed and when the old methods are dyin' out anyway.

MRS. CARRAWAY. All I can say is, they might 'ave waited till I'd died out !

FRED. They might 'ave waited for ever !

(MRS. CARRAWAY *and* FRED *regard each other unflinchingly*).

DOLLY. I 'ope old Mr. Fincher's comin' back before we 'ave to catch that train.

ROSE. I'm sure he will. He'd want to say goodbye. He's very

sorry about it all, and so am I. (*She looks at* FRED). (*He steadfastly picks a bone*). Sunny said first we lost the horses, then we got rid of the rabbits and now the Carraways are going. It's a pity it had to happen like this.

FRED. It can't be helped. (*He rises*).

ROSE. It really is too bad, Fred.

FRED. There we are!

ROSE. I wouldn't have thought it of you, Fred.

FRED. (*Banging down his fist*). I didn't buy the ruddy machine! Nobody consulted me about the arrangement! If Mr. Methews says we're to use the contraption—then use it we will! (*He walks away* U.R.)

(*The garden door opens and* MARY *enters. A few seconds later* NORMAN *enters, catching his foot and sprawling over the threshold*).

ROSE. (*Helping him up*). That silly old step!

NORMAN. Thank you.

ROSE. Doesn't seem like you'll ever get used to it.

NORMAN. Not now—no.

ROSE. Mary been showin' you round the farm?

MARY. I've been feeding the chicken.

NORMAN. I was having a look, yes. Mind you, I don't know very much about livestock.

MARY. Huh!

ROSE. I do think it's a pity you don't stay on, Mr. Bates. You'd find it very interestin' I'm sure.

NORMAN. Yes. I'd—I'd have liked to very much, but—

ROSE. Then whyever don't you?

FRED. Don't worry the lad, Rose.

MARY. Oh, Mr. Bates has lost interest in us, Mum.

NORMAN. I'd better catch the two-thirty, Mrs. Fincher.

ROSE. Oh dear. Aren't you two youngsters goin' into Maidstone after all?

MARY. (*Quickly*). No, Mum.

ROSE. But I thought you said, Mary, that—

NORMAN. (*Uncomfortably*). Well no, Mrs. Fincher. You see, when I thought I was staying here for a few weeks—

MARY. (*Interrupting angrily*). —he thought it would be worth his while cultivating me!

NORMAN. (*Horrified*). *No* Mary!

MARY. But now he's leaving anyway it looks like a waste of money!

ROSE. Mary, what an idea!

MARY. But it's true, isn't it, Mr. Bates? We may be country bumpkins but were not as slow as that!

DOLLY. You've got it all wrong, love.

MARY. Oh, no I haven't.

FRED. Mary! Shut up! The boy hasn't got the money to take you to Maidstone. He lent it to the Carraways.

DOLLY. That's right, dear. Bless 'is heart.

FRED. (*To* MARY). So you can stop this song and dance or I'll clip your ear for you!

ROSE. (*Bewildered*). But I thought—

FRED. He's got enough to get himself home and that's all.

NORMAN. I've got enough to pay *you*, Mrs. Fincher.

ROSE. Oh, that's all right, my dear.

MARY. (*Stormily*). Well, why didn't somebody tell me? (*To* NORMAN) Why didn't you say—you silly idiot!

(*She runs into the dining room*).

NORMAN. I'd better collect my things together.

(*With a look towards the dining room he goes upstairs*).

ROSE. That damned mechanical picker! (FRED *takes his cap and moves to the garden door*). Goin' out again, Fred?

FRED. I won't be long. Just goin' over to Four Crosses. I'll take the van.

(*He goes out*).

DOLLY. I think Ma's fallen asleep. It was that long walk this mornin', I suppose. She ought to know better.

MRS. CARRAWAY. (*Opening her eyes*). I can 'ear you!

DOLLY. Well, don't go and drop off. I don't fancy carryin' you to the station.

MRS. CARRAWAY. You? You couldn't carry a vote! You're not even ironin' them pleats properly.

DOLLY. I've got them all right.

MRS. CARRAWAY. 'Ere let me 'ave a go. (*She bustles up*).

DOLLY. Now sit down, Ma.

(MRS. CARRAWAY *takes iron*).

MRS. CARRAWAY. 'Aven't you got another iron? This one's stone cold.

ROSE. (*Taking irons from stove*). There're two more here, Mrs. Carraway, but don't you think—

MRS. CARRAWAY. (*Taking one and spitting on it*). That's better! Now then! (*She plonks it on the garment*). You'll find the good old-fashioned ways the best in the end. (*She irons away, murmuring to herself*). Mm. Well, of course, you've got some very funny material 'ere, 'aven't you? Where's that other iron?

ROSE. It's very hot, Mrs. Carraway.

MRS. CARRAWAY. That's what we need.

(*She changes irons and bangs down the new one*).

ROSE
DOLLY.
MRS. CARRAWAY. } (*As the material burns*). *Oh*!

DOLLY. Well, now you've given it a good old-fashioned scorch!

MRS. CARRAWAY. There's a funny thing!

(*They are all standing in a row, each holding an iron, in stunned silence.* SUNNY *enters from the garden, carrying a bag. He regards them*).

SUNNY. 'Allo! Practising yer 'andbells?

ROSE. What am I goin' to do for this afternoon? How can I get it out?

DOLLY. You'd better ask Ma! Ten to one she's got some good old-fashioned way—like rinsing it out in quicklime or something!

MRS. CARRAWAY. (*Brandishing her iron at* DOLLY). Don't you sauce me! You—

SUNNY. (*Dodging*). 'Ere! Stop flappin' them red-'ot irons about!

DOLLY. (*To* MRS. CARRAWAY). Sauce you! That's nothin' to what I'd like to do! (*Turning to* ROSE). I'm terribly sorry, Mrs. Fincher.

MRS. CARRAWAY. Well, so am I sorry. We're all sorry!

DOLLY. (*Turning on her*). But *you* did it! Honestly, Ma, I could—

MRS. CARRAWAY. If you hadn't been makin' such a mess of it—

DOLLY. *Me* makin' a mess! Why couldn't you keep your clumsy great mits off!

MRS. CARRAWAY. You mind your tongue!

DOLLY. I am, don't worry. If Mrs. Fincher weren't 'ere, I'd tell you what I'm really thinkin'.

MRS. CARRAWAY. You swear at me, you little cat, and you'll get this flatiron on yer 'ead. (*Flourishing it*).

DOLLY. And you'll get it back—with interest!

(*Flourishing hers*).

MRS. CARRAWAY. Listen to 'er. Listen to the way she talks to 'er poor old Mother. I'll murder 'er!

(*They charge at each other.* ROSE *and* SUNNY *make themselves scarce*).

ROSE. Dad! Separate them!

SUNNY. No fears!

MRS. CARRAWAY. (*Pursuing*). Come 'ere! I'll knock you into the middle of next week!

(*The two women dodge round each other fiercely. Suddenly* MRS. CARRAWAY *screams out*).

ROSE. Oh, Mrs. Carraway, are you burnt?

MRS. CARRAWAY. No, I've stubbed me toe!

(*She slumps into chair* L. *moaning and clasping her foot.* ROSE *retrieves the irons*).

DOLLY. Serves you damn well right! (*To* ROSE). Oh, I could kill 'er!

MRS. CARRAWAY. No. No. Give over, Doll. I've 'urt meself.

ROSE. It was an accident, I know. I just won't be able to play today, that's all.

DOLLY. Now don't panic, love. If we dabbed it out straight away it might 'elp. I'll do it for you. (*She takes the shorts.* ROSE *folds up ironing-board*).

ROSE. Bring it into the scullery.

MRS. CARRAWAY. (*Sincerely*). I'm sorry, dear.

ROSE. I know, Mrs. Carraway.

(DOLLY *exits into scullery*, ROSE *is following*).

SUNNY. Rose! Where's that hydrangea plant of yours. I've got somethin' for it.

ROSE. (*Indicating*). Over there.

SUNNY. (*Opening the bag*). Old 'Arry always says to bury a few bits of iron under hydrangea, it 'elps keep it's colour. (*He grabs the plant, uproots it, drops the contents of the bag into the pot and stuffs the plant back*).

There!

ROSE. Whatever are you doin'!

SUNNY. Just a few old nuts and bolts, gel. Do it good, they will.

ROSE. I should think you've killed it.

SUNNY. Well, that's that. (*He sits*).

ROSE. What have you been up to all the mornin'? I thought you were gettin' me some onions.

SUNNY. Well, I don't reckon ours are up to much this year. No good for showing.

ROSE. I don't care. I just want some to cook!

(DOLLY *re-appears in doorway*).

SUNNY. I'll 'ave to talk to old 'Arry—find out if the same thing's 'appened to 'is. Seems to me— (*Sits* D.L.)

ROSE. (*Losing patience*). Oh, why can't you do what I ask you. Old Harry this and Old Harry that! Your Old Harry's been passed on this three months or more!

(ROSE *immediately regrets her outburst. The three women look anxiously at* SUNNY. *He sits silent for a moment, then feels in his pocket.* ROSE *offers her own handkerchief, but* SUNNY *ignores it and it is his pipe that he eventually produces*).

SUNNY. Ah well. Old 'Arry didn't know much about onions anyway. (*He lights up*).

(*The three women relax,* ROSE *follows* DOLLY *out*).

The trouble with onions is, they're reckless feeders. Soot and salt. Fair gollop it up.

MRS. CARRAWAY. Do you mind? I've just finished my dinner.

SUNNY. Funny you enjoyin' it down 'ere like you do.

MRS. CARRAWAY. You don't 'ave to know 'ow to feed an onion to like a bit of fresh air now and again. I don't know why we stick in London at all—not now the Carraways are all scattered. There's no reason. You've got television down 'ere, 'aven't you?

SUNNY. Oh yes. Got it before we got the drains.

MRS. CARRAWAY. Mind you, it's cheerful in London. People to talk to all the time and that.

SUNNY. I don't reckon you need a lot of yappin' neighbours to keep you 'appy. Just a couple of you to keep each other company, you know.

MRS. CARRAWAY. Perhaps you're right. Provided it's someone you get on with all right and round about the same age, you know.

SUNNY. Mm. Don't reckon it matters much where you live if you've got the right kind of companionship.

MRS. CARRAWAY. That's true.

SUNNY. (*After a pause*). I've enjoyed our little chats together, Mrs. Carraway.

MRS. CARRAWAY. So 'ave I, Mr. Fincher.

SUNNY. Even if you 'ave only 'ad a couple of days 'ere.

MRS. CARRAWAY. (*Significantly*). Well, I haven't gone yet.

SUNNY. (*The same*). No more you 'aven't.

(NORMAN *comes down the stairs, he is carrying his bag and raincoat. At the bottom he sets them down*).

NORMAN. I covered the bed in. I—I don't know whether Mrs. Fincher wanted to take off my sheets.

MRS. CARRAWAY. Why? 'Ave you got somethin'?

NORMAN. No. I—er—

SUNNY. Rose'll see to it, son.

(MARY *appears*, D.R. *having heard his voice.* NORMAN *crosses to her*).

MARY. I'm sorry, Norman. I don't know what I said those things for. It was disappointment, I think.

NORMAN. It was my fault. I shouldn't have given the wrong impression. I don't know what I was ashamed of. I really needed the money!

MARY. It's—well—you didn't look like a hop-picker.

NORMAN. This is the first suit I've had since I was fifteen and I'm still paying my mother for it!

MARY. And you didn't *sound* right.

NORMAN. But that's just snobbery, Mary.

MARY. (*Indignantly*). It's not! It's snobbery when one of *your* sort won't accept *our* sort!

NORMAN. I'm not a 'sort'!

MARY. Oh, I'm sorry. Don't let's argue. It's nearly time for you to go!

NORMAN. Not yet.

MARY. We've hardly got to know each other.

NORMAN. It wasn't necessary. With some people you're friends as soon as you meet.

MARY. Did you feel that?

NORMAN. Look at the way we disagree! (*They laugh*). I'm coming down again, Mary, you know. Just as soon as I've got some cash. That is if you'd like me to.

MARY. When will you come?

NORMAN. (*Uncertainly*). We—ell—

MARY. I wish you could get a job down here.

NORMAN. Well, I'll have to finish training as a teacher, then training as a soldier, then—

MARY. Then train as a farmer!

NORMAN. But I don't know anything about animals or crops.

MARY. Well, what do you know about?

NORMAN. Machinery and chemicals—

MARY. But you're the very man!

NORMAN. But the animals and crops?

MARY. Oh *those*! (NORMAN *laughs*). But you'd love living here, Norman. If only you'd been staying you'd have found out. I could have shown you. Look across there! (*They move to window*).

NORMAN. (*Looking out*). All I can see is that infernal hop-picker.

MARY. On! (*She swings him round the other way*). There! It's even lovelier that way.

NORMAN. There's all the difference!

(*They gaze out of the window, talking quietly*).

SUNNY. Reckon there's a lot to be said for re-marriage between widows and widowers, you know.

MRS. CARRAWAY. Such as?

SUNNY. I mean while they've still got their faculties.

MRS. CARRAWAY. Still got 'em? I've got more now than I've ever 'ad.

SUNNY. I mean you can still cook and sew and that.

MRS. CARRAWAY. 'Ere now, wait a minute. I finished with all that lark years ago.

SUNNY. I don't think you've got the right approach, Mrs. Carraway.

MRS. CARRAWAY. Who says I'm approachin'? I'm retreatin', mate.

SUNNY. Wouldn't you like to be a housewife again?

MRS. CARRAWAY. What, after fifty years of it!

SUNNY. Wouldn't you like to 'ave a place of your own again and a 'usband?

MRS. CARRAWAY. Depends on the place and the 'usband.

SUNNY. Well, a little cottage round 'ere, say, and—er—someone like me for a 'usband. Just a thought crossin' my mind, you know.

MRS. CARRAWAY. Well, don't stop it.

SUNNY. You consider it, my gel. Make 'andsome couple we would. I've often thought of gettin' wed again,but there's not much of a field hereabouts. I fancied a lively sort with plenty of 'go', you know. After all, if we set up 'ouse, somebody would 'ave to do the work.

MRS. CARRAWAY. Well, what's wrong with you?

SUNNY. (*Mildly*). All right then. It's flyin' in the face of nature, but I'd do 'alf. There!

MRS. CARRAWAY. Are you any good at it?

SUNNY. I can peel spuds. Don't know much about anythin' else, maybe, but I can peel spuds, all right.

MRS. CARRAWAY. Mm. Nice varied diet we look like 'avin.

SUNNY. And what about our two pensions put together? Forty shillings and forty shillings, that's—

(*He begins calculating on his fingers, using them all up*).

MRS. CARRAWAY. All right, don't bother to take off your shoes, you're all wrong!

SUNNY. Eh?

MRS. CARRAWAY. Listen, mate, if I re-marry I lose me pension--

bang—like that! And we'd get twenty-five shillings to keep me instead.

SUNNY. (*Shaken*). Really? That makes quite a difference it's true, but I reckon—

MRS. CARRAWAY. Lookin' at the whole thing on a purely business footin', Mr. Fincher, you'd cost me fifteen shillings a week.

SUNNY. But, Mrs. Carraway—

MRS. CARRAWAY. I'm sorry, chum, but you're a luxury I can't afford.

SUNNY. It's nice of you to put it like that, but—

MRS. CARRAWAY. Oh, I've had me fifteen bob offers before, love. Dolly says I don't know the value of money, but I know a job lot when I see it!

SUNNY. I don't know that I like that.

MRS. CARRAWAY. For that matter I'm no bargain myself. Look, I'm not prepared to sacrifice my pension but I don't see why folks of our age should worry too much about gettin' married. If we want to live together for a bit of company I don't see why we shouldn't.

SUNNY. (*Deeply shocked*). Mrs. Carraway!

MRS. CARRAWAY. If that's 'ow you feel about it, I suppose you're right. Looks like you've 'ad it.

SUNNY. It's certainly something to think about.

(*They sink into silence.* MARY *and* NORMAN *move downstage*).

NORMAN. Well, it's certainly something to think about.

MARY. It looks as if there'll be plenty of time to think too. Why, some people are married at our age.

NORMAN. Oh, well, if you want to get married—

MARY. (*Delightedly astonished*). Yes?

NORMAN. You'd better let me know because it won't be worth my coming back, will it?

MARY. (*In a small voice*). No.

NORMAN. I hope you don't . . . . I mean . . . . I'd look forward to coming back—that is if you'd like me to.

MARY. Yes, I would. But I don't suppose you will. You'll marry some mistress in a primary school. It's people like you cause the shortage of teachers.

NORMAN. What do you keep talking about marriage for, Mary? Don't you read Evelyn Home? That's the way to scare a boy off!

MARY. (*Laughing*). You don't look very frightened.

NORMAN. I'm a smooth operator!

MARY. Don't give me that, Jackson!

(*They laugh.* MARY *catches sight of the clock*).

Oh gosh! Just look at the time!

NORMAN. And I don't seem to have seen anything of the farm at all. Hardly a cog or a test tube!

MARY. Let's go out. I'll show you the milking machine and the new pigs and the old barn.

NORMAN. The old barn sounds as if it might have possibilities.

MARY. Come on, Norman, take a last look round. That is if you'd like to.

NORMAN. Mary, why do we keep asking each other if we'd like to? We've only got fifteen minutes!

(*He takes her hand and they hurry out.* NORMAN *trips down the steps, but they carry on—laughing as they go*).

(SUNNY *and* MRS. CARRAWAY *gaze after them.* DOLLY *returns, bearing the shorts*).

DOLLY. I think it's going to be all right!

SUNNY. (*Eagerly*).
MRS. CARRAWAY. } What is?

DOLLY. Rose's shorts.

SUNNY.
MRS. CARRAWAY. } (*Sitting back*). Oh.

DOLLY. The scorch isn't goin' to show after all. Now then, Ma, you'd better start gettin' your coat on, you always take a year.

MRS. CARRAWAY. Well, if you'd sew me linin' up—Where is it anyway?

DOLLY. Over there! (*Indicating*).

ROSE. (*Entering*). I've just got time to change, then I'll see you to the station.

(*She hurries upstairs with the shorts*).

MRS. CARRAWAY. There's time enough yet.

ROSE. Don't go by the clock, Mrs. Carraway. It's wrong. (*She disappears.* DOLLY *and* MRS. CARRAWAY *start dressing helped by* SUNNY. MARY *and* NORMAN *rush in.* NORMAN *is looking at his watch. He leaps over the step*).

MARY. But are you sure your watch isn't fast?

NORMAN. Definitely not. That clock must be wrong!

DOLLY. It is, dear.

MARY. Oh gosh!

NORMAN. Will you give me a hand, Mary?

(*She helps him to strap odd items to his bag and tie some books together, while he struggles into a raincoat and fills the pockets with oddments*).

DOLLY. Did you give Phillip his seed, Ma?

MRS. CARRAWAY. No.

DOLLY. That's good. The journey on top might 'ave upset 'im.

MRS. CARRAWAY. (*Holding up cage*). He'll be happier with his cover on.

DOLLY. All right. All right. I'll get round to it in a minute.

MRS. CARRAWAY. Did you bring it down?

DOLLY. I don't know. Didn't you? (*She is still struggling with the luggage*).

MRS. CARRAWAY. I can't remember.

DOLLY. Oh, Ma! I'll slip up and 'ave a last look round.

(*She tears up the stairs*).

MRS. CARRAWAY. (*To* SUNNY *who is fumbling with her sleeve*). What are you doin'? 'Elpin' me with me coat or doin' the mambo?

SUNNY. It's a bit tight, isn't it?

MRS. CARRAWAY. It's slim-fittin'. Where's me 'at?

SUNNY. (*Handing it to her*). 'Ere you are. Ah!

(*He jumps as a pin pierces him*).

MRS. CARRAWAY. Mind the pin.

(DOLLY *comes part way down the stairs. There is a knock on the door and it is pushed open. A face peers round. It is a* FARMHAND).

FARMHAND. (*Calling*). Mrs. Fincher! Fred!

MARY. Dad's not here, Bill, and Mum's upstairs.

FARMHAND. (*Entering*). 'Allo Mary. 'Ave you 'eard about the mechanical picker over at Four Crosses? It's been got at!

(*Everyone registers interest*).

MARY. Got at?

FARMHAND. Early this morning. Couldn't make out why it wouldn't go, and guess what?

ALL. What?

FARMHAND. Something's been thrown in the works. They found a lot of wire spokes and bits of material, And, of all things, the handle of an umbrella.

DOLLY. An *umbrella*!

(MRS. CARRAWAY *removes her hat and begins unbuttoning her coat. Everyone begins talking at once*).

MARY. (*Running upstairs*). Mum! Mum!
NORMAN. An umbrella. How did that get in there?
FARMHAND. Funny thing, isn't it? You never 'eard the fuss.
DOLLY. Ma! Now I wonder—

MRS. CARRAWAY (*Innocently*). Maybe it was mine—someone found it in the ditch, perhaps.

SUNNY. An umbrella! That's a queer thing! That's very odd! (*With a troubled expression he moves to the hydrangea pot*).

MRS. CARRAWAY. (*To* FARMHAND). And it stopped the machine workin', did it?

FARMHAND. It did that all right!

NORMAN. (*Delighted*). Well!

(*Everyone begins undressing again.* ROSE *comes down the stairs, dressed for the stoolball match*).

MARY. Oh, Mum! The hop-picking machine's had an umbrella thrown in its works.

ROSE, (*To* FARMHAND). Oh my! Did it damage it?

FARMHAND. Pretty well nothin' left of it. Didn't hurt the machine though.

(*Those who have been busily undressing stop in their tracks*).

MARY. But I thought you said—

FARMHAND. Oh, it wouldn't have gone with that thing in it, of course, but they got all the bits out.

(MRS. CARRAWAY, DOLLY *and* NORMAN *begin to dress again*).

ROSE. So it's workin' all right is it ?

FARMHAND. No, that's what I came to tell you. There's a whole lot of nuts and bolts missin' off it as well.

NORMAN. Important ones ?

FARMHAND. Vital !

(*The three start undressing again.* SUNNY *crosses the room with the hydrangea pot*).

SUNNY. I reckon it's too warm for this in 'ere.

FARMHAND. The manager's goin' mad !

SUNNY. Maybe this would do better out in the garden.

ROSE. Oh, Dad, how can you worry about gardenin' at a time like this ? (*She takes the pot*). Put that silly plant down. Go and help Mrs. Carraway with her coat. We're goin' to need pickers after all.

FARMHAND. I don't know about that, Mrs. Fincher. They've sent to the engineers and it looks like it can be repaired in a day or two.

(DOLLY, MRS. CARRAWAY *and* NORMAN *fling on their coats and gather up their belongings once more*).

ROSE. (*To* FARMHAND). Have you told Fred about this ?

FARMHAND. No. I couldn't see him around. Thought 'e was 'ere.

ROSE. Well, never mind. I'll tell him when he comes in.

(FARMHAND *goes to the door*).

FARMHAND. Strange thing, wasn't it ? They reckon it was gypsies, you know, or maybe some of the boys from the reformatory. (*He goes*).

MARY. Well, whoever it was didn't make much of a job of it !

ROSE. But what a terrible thing to do ! Even if the owner is a millionaire.

DOLLY. We've got to get off if we're goin' to catch that train.

(*The three laden visitors move to the door*).

NORMAN. Goodbye, Mrs. Fincher, thanks for having me.

ROSE. Goodbye, lad, come down again soon.

NORMAN. Yes.

(*He takes* MARY'S *hand and quietly holds it while the others say their farewells*).

MRS. CARRAWAY. Take care of yourself, Mr. Fincher. And if you ever decide to come up to London—

SUNNY. And if *you* ever decide—

MRS. CARRAWAY. I'll let you know. Goodbye, Mrs. Fincher.

(*They shake hands with each other and at last set forth, with many a backward glance and dejected wave of the hand.* MARY, ROSE *and* SUNNY *see them off, then return to the room. They sit in melancholy silence.* ROSE *takes up her stoolball bat*).

ROSE. I ought to be going. (*She sighs*). I just don't feel like playin' today. (MARY *sighs*). I haven't the spirit in me to make a single cup of tea. (SUNNY *sighs*). Well, that's that. (MARY *and* SUNNY *sigh*).

(ROSE *sighs*).

(*The scullery door opens. In walks* MRS. CARRAWAY, *followed by* DOLLY, *followed by* NORMAN, *followed by* FRED. MARY, ROSE *and* SUNNY *are astounded*).

FRED. I found them all marchin' down to the station. Just stopped them, I did. Brought them through the yard.

ROSE. But—but why?

FRED. 'Aven't you 'eard? The mechanical picker's out of order. We're goin' to need all the hands we can get. No matter whose.

(*Everyone cheers*).

ROSE. But, Fred. Have you seen, Bill?

FRED. I saw Bill all right, and I've been over to Four Crosses.

ROSE. But can't they repair it?

FRED. Very likely, in time, but me and Mr. Methews think the machine's too unreliable!

MRS. CARRAWAY. I told you they'd need us!

(*She undoes her coat*).

ROSE. Oh, I'm so glad! I feel I could win this afternoon's match all on my own!

DOLLY. And we'll come down and cheer you!

NORMAN. We certainly will. Eh, Mary?

MARY. O.K. If we all go, maybe they'll give her an innings!

ROSE. Just dump your luggage and we'll sort it out later.

SUNNY. Mrs. Carraway and me'll go on. Come along, my dear, I'll show you the way.

MRS. CARRAWAY. That's right. (*She takes his arm*). Let's get crackin', old man. (SUNNY *totters to the door*). Oh crickey! See you down on the green in a couple of days' time. Dolly! Grab 'old of 'is other flipper. (*They go out*).

NORMAN. Thanks for the reprieve, Mr. Fincher. Come on, Mary.

(*He moves to the door*).

ALL. Mind the step!

NORMAN. Thanks!

MARY. You take *my* arm! (*Together they exit*).

ROSE. Isn't it lovely to see them all so happy, Fred?

FRED. (*Agreeing*). Mm. Rosie, reckon I'll watch you go through your paces myself.

(*He helps her with her coat*).

ROSE. (*Pleased and surprised*). Fred!

(*They move to the door*).

Fred, what did happen to the hop-machine? There seems to be some difference of opinion.

FRED. The conveyor belt was severed right through.

ROSE. (*Amazed*). The conveyor belt! Not the umbrella or the missing nuts and bolts?

FRED. No. It was the conveyor belt finished it.

ROSE. How awful! That wonderful machine!

FRED. Yes. Sheer vandalism! (*He goes through door then turns back*). AND IT WAS THE DEVIL'S OWN JOB CUTTIN' THROUGH IT. (*He goes out*).

(ROSE, *opened mouthed, follows as—*

THE CURTAIN FALLS).

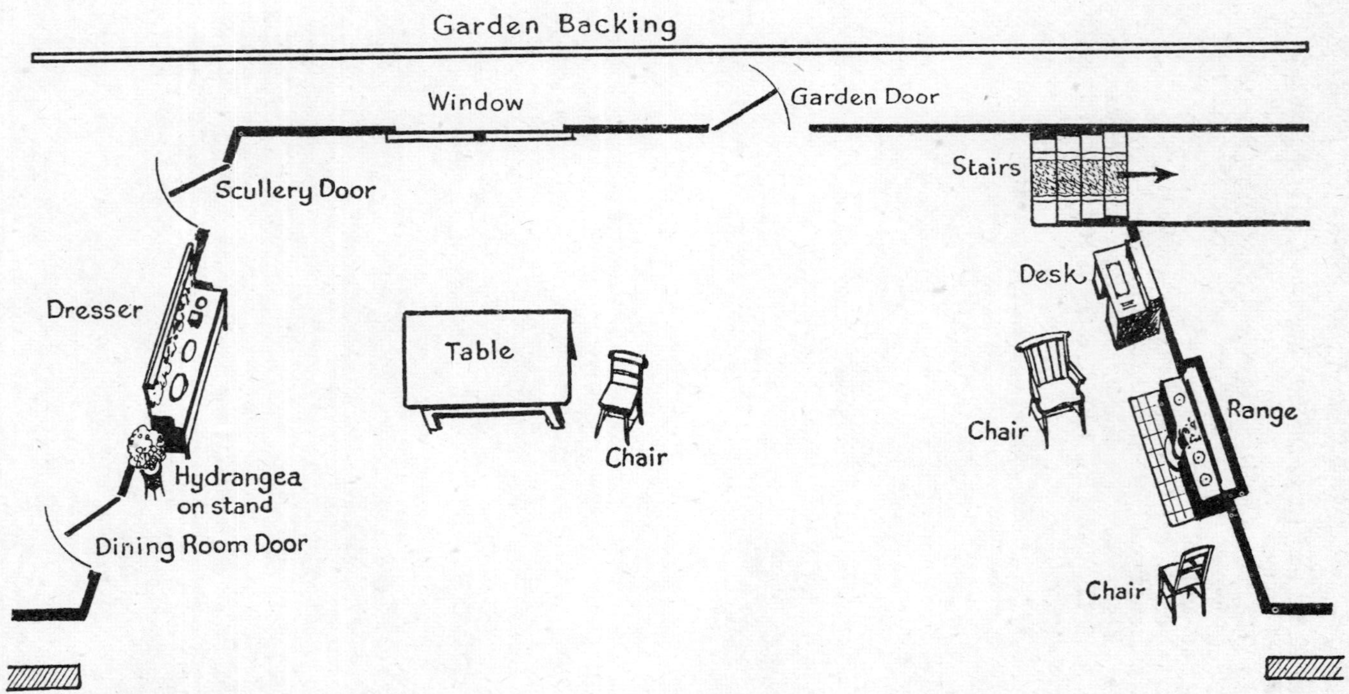

Garden Backing
Window
Garden Door
Stairs
Scullery Door
Desk
Dresser
Table
Chair
Range
Chair
Hydrangea
on stand
Chair
Dining Room Door
Chair

NOTES

NOTES

NOTES

Printed in Great Britain by
Whitstable Litho Ltd., Whitstable, Kent